Mountaineering

John Cleare

Mountaineering

BLANDFORD PRESS

Poole   Dorset

First published in the U.K. 1980

Copyright © 1980 Blandford Press Ltd.,
Link House, West Street,
Poole, Dorset, BH15 1LL

British Library Cataloguing in Publication Data

Cleare, John
  Mountaineering.
  1. Mountaineering
  I. Title
  796.5'22   GV200

ISBN 0 7137 0946 4 (Hardback edition)
ISBN 0 7137 1082 9 (Paperback edition)

Phototypeset in Monophoto Apollo
by Oliver Burridge and Co. Ltd.

Printed in Hong Kong by South China Printing Co.

Contents

1
Mountains and Men

'Men go out to wonder at the Mountain Heights'
St Augustine: 'Confessions' — 399 A.D.

From the very beginning man has gazed up with mixed emotions at the mountains which have barred his path or formed the horizon of his civilisations. 'A hill of impressive height,' is how the Oxford Dictionary defines a mountain. There are no other rules it seems—it is enough that a mountain should engender awe. The Hindu sages and Chinese philosophers derived sublime inspiration from sight of the eternal snows and even the hardened western traveller cannot fail to identify with the mountain reverence of the gentle Himalayan Bhuddists. There is something moving and mystical about the flags that flutter their prayers to the wind on the high pass, about the chortens silhouetted against the ice-hung horizon, about the spectacular situations where gompa and monastery hang between earth and sky.

It is easy to understand how mountains, so unapproachable, their summits so far above the plane of man's own existence, should themselves become sacred. It was only natural that many should become the homes of a wide range of assorted deities, and specific gods and goddesses have been known to inhabit such diverse summits as Olympus in Greece, Kailas in Tibet, Mt Kenya in Africa and Mt Sinai in Egypt— among others. In some cases they still do. The Navajo Nation have barred access to the clustered spires of New Mexico's Shiprock, and lovely Machapuchare (Plate 1), rising resplendent before Annapurna's crystal wall, its summit approached but never reached, is now forbidden in deference to local wishes. This 'sacred relationship' does not necessarily inhibit climbing however. The ancient Japanese Shugendo concept, for instance, teaches that sacred power is attainable high on a mountain, while 600 years ago the Incas of the Atacama Andes were placing altars —and burials—on 20,000 foot (6000 m) summits. However, mountaineering as a sport and practised just for fun has been in existence for not much more than a century.

Not everywhere were the mountains so benevolent. The alpine peasant of medieval Europe could have derived little spiritual satisfaction from the mountains that encircled his horizon and which he knew by such names as Eiger (Ogre), Mont Maudit (Accursed Mountain) or Teufelsberg (Devil's Mountain). Even enlightened scholars knew that they were infested with dragons and demons, with trolls and hobgoblins. King Peter III of Aragon, in the thirteenth century, met a 'horrible dragon of enormous size' on the summit of Pyrenean Pic Canigou and it was not until 1585 that the undead Pontius Pilate was banished from his little lake high on Mount Pilatus above Lucerne. Even in 1864 it was the Spirits of the Damned who hurled the daily rock-fall from the Matterhorn. How otherwise could simple folk explain the inexplicable? What were such common mountain phenomena as thunder and lightning, avalanche, St Elmo's Fire or the mysterious Brocken Spectre that floats in the mist-filled abyss (Plate 2), if not supernatural? What was Ferlas Mhor, the Great Grey Man, who prompted Norman Collie—the scientist and famous mountaineer—to flee for his life on Ben Macdhui? What is the Yeti (Plate 4), or Alma, or Sasquatch, the mysterious creature that inhabits mountain wilderness across the Asian and North American continents? Not only Soviet scientists but many western mountaineers—including myself—have encountered sufficient evidence to indicate that he, at least, is something more than mere superstition. The fact is that mountains are neither benign or malevolent. They are the same yesterday as they will be tomorrow. Man may climb mountains but he can never 'conquer' them, the very word is out of context for how can man subdue a mountain? Mountains are merely beautiful or awesome and the only conquest by the climber is that of himself.

The relationship of a mountaineer to his mountains is a very subjective one, a very esoteric one, and by mountaineer I mean anyone who takes seriously to the mountains in a wide variety of ways, many of which we shall examine in Chapter 5. Men—and women—seek different things from their mountains and if their involvement is close enough they will almost certainly find that which they seek. Enjoyment is a personal thing and in pushing ourselves towards our own limit—whatever that limit maybe—we experience something deep and lasting. The nature of the challenge against which me measure ourselves, its size or its scale, is unimportant.

For mountain people however, the relationship is different: few climb for fun. Mountaineering tends to be the sport of the visiting lowlander, highlanders must be more pragmatic. The value to the shepherd of his high mountain pastures is obvious (Plate 14) and so is the importance of the little mountain hyrax to the Bakonjo hunters of the Ruwenzori (Plate 12). To the Tamang porter the mountain trails of the Himalaya are a freeway to affluence while even the sherpas, those most accomplished of mountain people, do not climb for fun although they certainly enjoy their work (Plates 13, 15). The yeti himself, the so-called Abominable Snowman, only crosses the high snows to reach the next valley. It is interesting to note that several of the keen climbers who have moved out of the cities in recent years to live and work in mountain areas, have since given up climbing! Perhaps mountaineering is something of an 'escape'?

Mountaineering has been defined as 'the crossing of potentially dangerous mountain or other steep terrain, in safety'. Danger and safety are key words: the former because it is the raison d'etre—but never the substance—of the game, the second because it is mountaineering's only justification. A dangerous mountaineer is a bad mountaineer. A good mountaineer will know fear, indeed he will probably enjoy its stimulation, but it will never be uncontrolled or reasonless fear. To use a nautical analogy, which is more apt than it might seem because mountaineering and ocean sailing have much in common, he will delight in sailing close to the wind knowing he is in perfect control. But how wide the ocean, how rough the sea and just how close to the wind, are conscious and personal choices—it is enough that he is at sea. Mountains are all things to all men and what is dangerous to one may not be so to another. The danger, and the challenge, depend on experience and ability or just plain inclination.

Certainly mountaineering is an anarchistic sport. Unlike most other sports it does not depend on organisations and officials, competition and referees. It has no rules and its methods and outcome are of importance only to the participants themselves. Indeed many mountaineers would object to the label 'sport' for so esoteric a pastime but would find it difficult to substitute a different word, although its ethic is truer to the original meaning of the word than any Olympic sport. A university research project carried out a few years ago on a group of some hundred high-standard alpinists showed that all were highly individualistic and usually successful people talented also in another quite different field. Typically they were resentful of authority. Perhaps these are qualities that one might expect from top-class exponents of a sport whose rewards are abstract, in which the responsibility for one's actions are entirely one's own, and in which mistakes can earn the ultimate penalty. Possibly it is indicative of the appeal of mountaineering.

So what is mountaineering about? The following chapters might, I hope, with some reading between the lines, start to answer that question, although it is impossible, in this little book, to do more than generalise. Much, anyway, will always remain personal for, as Sir Leslie Stephen—President of the Alpine Club in 1866 and one of the most eminent literary critics of his time—declared: 'The mountaineer has learnt a language which is but partially revealed to ordinary men.' I have been climbing for thirty years and I have experienced many things the ordinary man would understand and many he would not.

Any sportsman would understand the physical exultation of moving fast, for in the Alps speed is safety, up the 3000 feet (900 m) of arcing rock slabs that is the North East Face of the Piz Badile. The delight of moving in perfect control close to the limits of one's ability—up and up and up. The delight in being alive amid this stupendous rock architecture. The delight in friendship and the all trusting companionship of the rope. Would he understand the necessary pre-dawn start with the body fighting sleep and the stomach fighting fear and the sweat running cold in the small of the back?

A tortured river of ice a mile long and half a mile high, the Khumbu Ice-fall of Mount Everest is not a pleasant place. A dozen men have died in it. But it is strangely beautiful, its terrifying silence occasionally broken by the rumble of crumbling ice. The memory of several five-hour climbs through the Ice-fall is, in retrospect, a worthwhile one though I did not enjoy them at the time for the danger was, I considered, outside my control. I suspect that only a fellow climber would appreciate that particular experience.

Many people could share my elation on a small Himalayan peak, it was only a small one—9000 feet (3000 m) lower than Everest—but it was my first virgin summit. We had been climbing steadily and continuously since dawn, just the two of us. We had forced a difficult face, traversed a series of gendarmes and climbed a long and steepening snow crest. Always the summit remained ahead and time slipped by unnoticed. Then came an awkward ice pitch. Balanced on my front points I carefully wound in a screw and clipped through the rope. Above was a steep ice bulge. I pulled over it and there was nothing beyond. Just a void of blue shadow and a blood red sun dropping into a sea of distant peaks. The summit was tiny but it was ours. The last colour fled westward before the cloak of the night. We were alone with the rising moon. We knew we faced an epic descent down an unknown ice-arete by moonlight. Our elation was heady and laced with fear. But fear of what? We were partners of the rope and there was deep trust between us. Can friendship offer more?

2
Mountains of the World

Mountains, large and small, rise on every continent. While it is not strictly true that mountains are as important as the men who climb them, certain of the world's mountains are of far less importance than their height or extent might suggest. This could be because they offer nothing to the climber or, more typically, because access to them is made difficult or even impossible for political reasons: here the great ranges of Central Asia come to mind, almost forgotten behind iron and bamboo curtains. Conversely mere hills blessed with good crags may take on a status that belies their size if they are easily accessible lungs for large centres of population or if the men who frequent them have— or still do—shape world mountaineering. A classic example is the English Lake District.

Europe
Even today, when the achievements and development of mountaineering are as likely to be dominated by men, and women, from Tokyo and Seattle as from Munich or Manchester, Europe is still the home—the crucible even—of mountaineering. Here were invented all the mountain sports that we shall examine later and these were nurtured to maturity by European exponents.

Europe is dominated by the Alps, the best known, best documented and most climbed upon mountains on earth. Their great chain, some 600 miles (950 km) long and around 80 miles (130 km) wide, arcs from the Mediterranean coast behind Monaco, through Central Europe to fade into the Balkans, one or other of the several crests forming the natural frontiers between the alpine nations. Practically and geographically the Alps may be divided into many separate ranges, each of different character and appeal. The higher are usually composed of igneous rocks and hold heavy glaciation, the lower or peripheral ranges are mostly limestone. Climbing and skiing have been developed and climbing huts abound everywhere but it is still possible, with diligence, to escape into relatively unfrequented and wild mountain country.

The South Western Alps cover the first 150 miles (250 km) northward from the sea. Initially the almost sub-tropical Maritimes form a group of sharp little rock peaks reaching 10,000 feet (3000 m) before the less

10

notable Cottians and Graians line the main crest. West of the crest, in France, rises the important Dauphiné Massif, a desolate glaciated region of large craggy mountains, no less than 23 of them topping 12,000 feet (3650 m), and famed for their rock routes. Though not the highest summit, La Meije (13,068 ft/3983 m) is one of the great peaks of the Alps. The impressive ice-hung Cogne Massif—or Eastern Graians—springs from a spur north-eastwards in Italy, and offers several classic snow and ice climbs on such peaks as the Gran Paradiso (13,323 ft/4061 m) and Grivola.

Now the chain bends eastwards into the Mont Blanc Massif, the most important single group in the Alps. The great snow dome of Mont Blanc itself, highest point in Europe west of the Caucasus, throws down a magnificent 11,000 foot (3300 m) face of rock and ice into Italy and is surrounded by avenues of spectacular and jagged lesser peaks cradling long valley glaciers descending into France—most famous of which is the 7½ mile (12 km) long Mer de Glace. Chamonix and Courmayeur are the French and Italian climbing centres respectively and the far eastern end of the massif lies in Switzerland. Many of the peaks are of world renown, among them the Grandes Jorasses (13,799 ft/4208 m), Les Droites (13,123 ft/4000 m), the Aiguille du Dru (12,316 ft/3754 m) and the many-pinnacled ridge of the Chamonix Aiguilles, one of which is Le Grépon (11,424 ft/3482 m). Superb red granite and a series of fine ice walls have provided over 2000 guidebooked climbs, of all grades and of great quality and character, while aggressive and competitive climbers have made the Massif the crucible of modern alpinism.

Over the Great St Bernard Pass the Pennine Alps stretch for over 80 miles (130 km) along the Swiss/Italian frontier. Here stand ten of the twelve highest Alpine peaks, typically aloof and alone. Around Zermatt, surely the world's most famous mountain resort, cluster such splendid summits as the Matterhorn (14,688 ft/4476 m), Monte Rosa (15,203 ft/4633 m)—Switzerland's highest, Dom (14,911 ft/4544 m), Weisshorn (14,780 ft/4504 m) and Dent Blanche (14,295 ft/4357 m), noted, as are the other Pennine peaks, for their long classic climbs on mixed ground—climbs of serious mountaineering interest rather than great technical difficulty. A sequence of high interconnected glaciers provide excellent ski-touring and ski-mountaineering in winter.

A knot of formidable ice-draped peaks rising above a tangle of great glaciers is the main feature of the Bernese Alps which parallel the Pennines north of the deep Rhône Valley. Thirty seven rise above 12,000 feet (3660 m) while the Aletsch is the longest glacier in the Alps (15½ miles/25 km). The Finsteraarhorn (14,022 ft/4274 m)—the highest summit—stands remote in the middle of the knot and better known are the line of peaks which form the 'Oberland', the northern wall of the Range, overlooking the celebrated resorts of Grindlewald, Mürren and Kandersteg and the plains of north-west Europe beyond, among them the Eiger (13,036 ft/3970 m), the Mönch (13,448 ft/4099 m) and the Jungfrau (13,642 ft/4158 m) (Plate 23). Although the weather is notoriously poor and the rock often bad, the Range is noted for its classic climbs on mixed ground and for the largest concentration of great ice routes in the Alps.

The mountain crests of the Western Alps continue into eastern Switzerland to become the Central Alps, embracing the headwaters of the Rhine. Most of the mountains are fairly small and the region is noted more for winter ski-touring and mountaineering than for summer climbing. The notable exception is the cluster of impressive peaks that surround the Dammastock (11,906 ft/3628 m) in the west of the region and from whose glaciers rises the infant Rhône. Among these the superb Salbitschijen (9780 ft/2980 m) with its many-towered aretes of immaculate granite is justly renowned but there is much excellent rock climbing on other peaks in the vicinity as well.

Ranged along the Italian frontier in the far south-eastern corner of Switzerland stand the compact Bregaglia and Bernina Groups. The former, a chain of wild granite peaks and jagged ridges rising above small glaciers, is famous for its rock-climbs—many ranking with the best in the Alps. The Piz Badile—(10,853 ft/3308 m) with its classic 3000 foot (900 m) North East Face—is one of the Alps' great mountains but there are also several ice climbs of note, the North Face of splendid Monte Dizgrazia (12,067 ft/3678 m) the highest summit, for instance, isolated on a spur into Italy. By contrast the adjoining Bernina peaks are entirely ice-hung and several large glaciers flow from them towards the smart resort of St Moritz in the Engadin, the valley of the new-born Inn, at their feet. Piz Bernina (13,284 ft/4049 m) is the most easterly 4000 metre peak in the Alps and close by stand Piz Roseg and Piz Palu, both flaunting north faces of some reputation. Typically the climbs in the area are snow-and-ice routes of medium grade but great quality.

Filling most of Austria and much of north-east Italy with mountains, the Eastern Alps form the final 250 miles (400 km) of the Range. Here there are three parallel lines of mountains, each of very different character, the central one continuing the main alpine crest eastwards with the major icy peaks rising from it. The highest summits of the Italian Ortler and the frontier Ötztal groups rise well above 12,000 feet (3700 m) with the Stubai and Zillertal only slightly lower. These groups form the South and North Tirol. Austria's highest peak, the magnificent Grossglockner (12,461 ft/3798 m), rises from the extensive Hohe

Tauern group where some fifty other summits top 10,000 feet (3000 m). The larger peaks of all these groups are known for their fine routes on ice, snow and mixed ground but there are also excellent rock climbs particularly in the spiky Zillertal and the region is ideal for winter climbing and ski mountaineering.

Northward lies the chain of the Kalkalpen—the Northern Limestone Ranges—relatively small but wild and craggy rock peaks, snowless in summer, running along the Bavarian frontier and beyond. Here are the Wetterstein, where stands the Zugspitze (9718 ft/2962 m), Germany's highest summit; the Karwendal, at whose feet lies Innsbruck, the lovely capital of the Tirol; the Wilde Kaiser and the Dachstein: mountains renowned as the forcing ground of modern alpine rock-climbing. Southward runs the chain of the Dolomite, Carnic and Julian Alps. Extending over 80 miles (130 km) the Dolomites are a confusion of dramatic limestone spires and imposing yellow walls. Cortina is the famous resort in this beautiful region which is a paradise for high standard rock-climbers. Invariably routes are steep and exposed and often actually overhanging and those on such features as the huge 2000 foot (600 m) South Face of the Marmolata (10,965 ft/3342 m), the 3 mile (5 km) long North West Face of the Civetta and the outward leaning north walls of the Tre Cime di Lavaredo are of world repute. The Julians, culminating in Trigalev (9393 ft/2863 m), Yugoslavia's highest summit, offer good limestone climbing, but they are the final knot of the long Alpine chain. As varied a range as any on earth, the Alps offer almost everything the mountain lover could desire.

Isolating Spain from the rest of Europe, the 270 mile (430 km) range of the Pyrenees is lower and less extensive than the Alps. More than fifty peaks rise above 10,000 feet (3000 m) of which the highest is Pico Aneto (11,168 ft/3404 m). Several tiny glaciers still cling to the steep northern flanks of the range while summer snow cover is small. Most moutains are either granite or limestone and it is this latter rock that forms the great cliff-girt cirques and sensational waterfalls that so characterise the region: it is one of outstanding beauty and much of it is still wild and remote country. The ascent of any Pyrenean summit is little more than a scramble but there is fine rock-climbing throughout the range for which the massive Vignemale and the sharp Pic du Midi d'Ossau are well known, and there is also some of the world's best pot-holing. It is ideal country for hill-walking and scrambling and—in winter—for nordic ski touring.

Europe's most extensive mountain system lies in Norway. Complex and extending over 1000 miles (1600 km) behind an incredibly indented coast, its highest summits just top 8000 feet (2400 m) but nearly 300 of them rise above 6000 feet (1800 m). There are several vestigial ice caps—including the largest in Europe, the Jostadals Breen—and many small glaciers, yet the proximity of the warm Gulf Stream ensures that even those mountains north of the Arctic Circle enjoy a relatively mild summer climate. Mountaineering is hardly alpine but steep rock abounds, most of it granite, typically as spiky peaks such as formidable Store Skagastølstind (7888 ft/2404 m), or as great cliffs like the famous Troll Wall in Romsdal, plumb vertical for over 4000 feet (1200 m). While there are no longer virgin summits there are plenty of unknown crags and faces particularly in the remote areas of the north.

Despite its small scale, Britain has much to offer the mountain lover besides many of mountaineering's historical associations. The north and west are predominantly hilly and the extremely diverse geology ensures that rock-climbing of some kind is never far away, whether on outcrops such as the famous gritstone edges of the Pennines (Plate 45) or on the miles of superb sea-cliffs that line the coast (Plates 42, 44). Rock-climbing in Britain is as highly developed as anywhere in the world. The rugged mountains of North Wales rise no higher than Snowdon (3560 ft/1085 m) or the more gentle Lake District fells than Scafell Pike (3210 ft/978 m) (Plate 17), but they hold a vast diversity of climbs on ancient volcanic rocks, besides excellent scrambling and hill-walking. Northward a tangle of rugged mountains extend for more than 200 miles (300 km) to form the Scottish Highlands. Once heavily glaciated but now holding virtually no summer snow despite an 'arctic-alpine' climate, these mountains exhibit a rich variety of form and structure: Ben Nevis is the highest summit at 4406 feet (1343 m). Most summits are easily accessible, though maybe remote, the notable exception being the jagged peaks of the Hebridean island of Skye, which together with Glencoe and Ben Nevis, offer the most popular rock-climbing. There is vast scope for scrambling and hill-walking but the Highlands are renowned for their winter mountaineering. Technical ice-climbs as hard as any in the world are found on such superb cliffs as those of Ben Nevis, Creag Meaghaidh (Plate 50) and the Cairngorms. Huge sea-cliffs in the remote western and northern isles have given almost expedition-ary climbs and the Old Man of Hoy sea-stack off Orkney is famous (Plate 43).

As in Britain, good climbing can be found elsewhere in Europe out-side the major moutain ranges, especially in such upland regions as the Ardennes, the Eifel, the Erzgebirge south of Dresden and the Calanques near Marseille. The small mountains of the Abruzzi Appennines 60 miles (100 km) east of Rome, where the limestone Gran Sasso massif rises to 9616 feet (2930 m), and the lovely and remote peaks of Corsica

(Monte Cinto—8890 ft/2710 m) are especially worthy of the climber's attention. Of most importance however are the Tatra, the highest of the long Carpathian chain, a compact and rugged massif astride the Czecho-slovak/Polish frontier. Ten sharp summits of naked granite top 8500 feet (2590 m) in the culminating High Tatra group and high crags fall from jagged ridges into deep corries cradling beautiful tarns. There is excellent summer rock climbing while heavy winter snows provide superlative snow-and-ice routes of similar style to those of Scotland. The finest expedition is the rarely completed winter traverse of the High Tatra, some 30 miles (50 km) of sustained climbing with a dozen bivouacs! The Tatra are the popular training ground for the powerful Polish and Czech climbers who figure prominently in world moun-taineering.

The final major European range is the Caucasus: while lying entirely in the USSR, its long and narrow crest is taken as the geographical boundary between Europe and Asia. Although the major peaks are some 3000 feet (900 m) higher, the Caucasus are comparable to the Alps in character and extent but with a loftier snow-line and rather smaller glaciers. The 160 mile (250 km) central section is the most interesting. Elbrus (18,481 ft/5633 m), the highest summit in Europe, is an easily ascended extinct volcano and is atypical. More characteristic are form-idable rock and ice peaks such as twin-fanged Ushba (15,453 ft/4710 m), jagged Dykh-Tau (17,074 ft/5204 m) or Shkhara (17,064 ft/5201 m) with its 6000 foot (1800 m) North Face falling to the Bezingi Basin—most famous of a series of such great glacier cirques. The important climbs tend to be long mixed routes and sometimes the multi-day traverses favoured by the Russians—as serious and committing as anything in the Alps but at higher altitude and in less stable weather. Although pio-neered by British and later Austrian and German climbers, the Caucasus is today virtually a Russian preserve. Technical standards are very high but all mountaineering is strictly regulated and few westerners care to brave the necessary bureaucracy to visit these superb mountains.

North America

Mountains—some of them great and worthy ranges—sweep north-wards through the republics of Central America, through Mexico, the United States and Canada, to fill Alaska, occupying almost the entire western third of North America. The great volcanoes of Mexico such as Citlaleptl (18,700 ft/5700 m), the third highest summit on the continent, and Popocateptl (17,888 ft/5452 m) are regularly ascended by straight-forward snow routes, but good technical climbs have been made on the rocky peaks and cliffs of Baja California and the Sierra Madre which, although rarely rising over 10,000 feet (3000 m), form the backbone of the country. North of the border the Sierra rise again as the Rockies, the major mountain chain and the continental divide of both the USA and Canada. Another great chain parallels the Pacific coast: the Sierra Nevada and the Cascades extend into Canada as the Coast Mountains. Between these chains rise the lesser mountains of the Great Basin.

The American Rockies comprise many consequent ranges of very different character. The largest is the Colorado Rockies where numerous sub-ranges form a complex tangle of typically rounded and scree-covered peaks, with occasional tiny glaciers lingering in their craggy corries, 53 of which rise above 14,000 feet (4267 m). The ascent of many summits, including the highest—Mt Elbert (14,433 ft/5399 m)—is an easy hike but there is excellent climbing on other peaks, particularly in the San Juan, Elk and Sangre de Cristo groups, where there are several technically difficult summits. Longs Peak (14,256 ft/4349 m) in the Front Range is world famous for its big wall routes and there is much very accessible crag climbing close to the cities of Boulder, Colorado Springs and elsewhere.

In the centre of Wyoming a narrow line of shattered granite peaks— the Wind River Range—stretch 100 miles (160 km) through a beautiful and remote wilderness. At the northern end Gannett Peak (13,785 ft/ 4202 m) and seven other 13,500 foot (4115 m) summits hold small glaciers but the smaller and more jagged rock peaks with their charac-teristic knife-edge aretes that lie southward give some of the best mountain rock-climbs in the land. The Cirque of the Towers is famous.

Also in Wyoming stand the Tetons, the most popular mountains in the USA. Dominated by the imposing Grand Teton (13,766 ft/4196 m) with its 6000 feet (1800 m) of vertical relief, this extremely accessible small group of spiky alpine rock-peaks, hung with diminutive glaciers, holds a profusion of splendid climbs, some actually on ice, and has been an important crucible of American mountaineering.

Idaho—a largely wilderness state—also contains notable mountains. The most important range is the Sawtooths, a fine and accessible group of granite aiguilles giving excellent routes. Climbs have also been made in the Lost River Range where Borah Peak (12,665 ft/3860 m) is the state's highest summit. Almost everywhere the Rockies hold something to delight the hiker, the scrambler, the climber or the cross-country skier.

The summits of Utah and Nevada rise over 13,000 feet (4000 m) and those of Arizona well over 12,000 feet (3800 m). They provide some good rock and some of the best powder skiing in the world, but it is the desert features of the Great Basin States that are unique. Sensational and difficult climbs have been made on the incredible sandstone spires and monoliths of such places as Zion, Monument Valley and Canyonlands (Plate 31). Great White Throne, the Totem Pole, Fisher Towers and the volcanic plug of Shiprock—just into New Mexico—are justly famed.

Mt Whitney (14,494 ft/4418 m), the highest summit in the 48 States, rises in California's Sierra Nevada, a beautiful range of serrated granite peaks with wild cirques, alpine meadows and a myriad small lakes. Scores of summits top 13,000 feet (4000 m) and there are some 60 tiny glaciers. Eastward the main crest rises steeply over 10,000 feet (3000 m) from the arid Owens Valley. The scope for technical rock-climbing, hiking and ski-touring is enormous while most summits can be reached by easy scrambling. Yet it is for the spectacular Yosemite Valley that the Sierra is world famous (Plate 30): such features as the 2900 foot (885 m) vertical wall of El Capitan and the awesome faces of Half Dome and other tremendous granite cliffs were the birthplace of big wall climbing.

Two very different mountain types characterise the Cascades of the Pacific Northwest. Aloof, isolated and glacier-draped, Mounts Rainier (14,408 ft/4392 m) and Hood (11,234 ft/3424 m)—the highest summits in Washington and Oregon respectively—are among the region's ten major volcanoes, while the 'North Cascades' are a complex of several hundred rugged and upstanding rock-peaks. Although they rarely top 9000 feet (2700 m) these latter are hung with ice-fields and glaciers and are the most alpine mountains in the contiguous USA. Access to the volcanoes, of which Rainier in particular holds a notable series of ice routes of all standards, is easy but approaches to the more remote of the alpine peaks are bedevilled by bush-choked valleys and poor weather. The climbing however, on rock, ice or mixed ground, can be of exceptional quality. Mention should also be made of the compact and heavily glaciated Olympic Range on the coast west of Puget Sound. Noted for hiking and easy climbing, these mountains rise to 7954 feet (2424 m) on Mt Olympus.

But there are mountains too, the low and gentle Appalachian Chain, in the eastern United States. These rounded hills, typically wooded to their summits except in New England, extend from Georgia to Maine and good rock-climbing is found on scattered crags everywhere. Especially notable are the 1000 foot (300 m) granite face of Cannon Mountain in New Hampshire and the winter climbing on Mt Washington (6288 ft/1917 m) nearby. The hiking trails of the Appalachians are famous and the highest top is Mt Mitchell (6684 ft/2037 m) in North Carolina.

A profusion of mountains fills the wilderness that is western Canada. The great wall of the Canadian Rockies rises abruptly from the Alberta prairies: barely 50 miles (80 km) across, it extends nearly 500 miles (800 km) north from the American frontier. Of hundreds of peaks more than 50 exceed 11,000 feet (3300 m) some are massive, some tower-like and some rise like huge shark fins. Typically they are ice-hung, displaying steep walls of markedly stratified sedimentary rock and cradling substantial glaciers. They tower above wide forested valleys with colourful lakes and large rivers. Mt Robson (12,972 ft/3954 m) the monarch of the Rockies (Plate 27), is a formidable peak of world stature and other famous peaks include Alberta, Assiniboine (Plates 25, 55, 57) and Edith Cavell. Access to some mountains, especially those surrounding the 150 square mile (325 sq.km) Columbia Ice Fields and the Lake Louise/Moraine Lake cirques, is very easy and top quality alpine climbs of all standards—but predominantly on snow, ice or mixed ground—abound. Difficult ascents of great north faces are a modern trend.

The line of the Rockies rises again some 250 miles (400 km) northward as the remote Lloyd George Range (9800 ft/2987 m) and, on the Yukon/Northwest Territories march, as the Selwyn and MacKenzie Mountains. Here, in the Logan Group, the 2400 foot (730 m) granite wall of elegant Lotus Flower Tower in the 'Cirque of the Unclimbables' is especially noteworthy.

Westwards across the Columbia River the Interior Ranges of British Columbia, the Purcells, the Selkirks, the Monashees and the Cariboos—heavily glaciated alpine mountains composed of a variety of rocks—parallel the Rockies. The first two ranges are the most important and, in this densely forested country, the least inaccessible. The highest summit is massive Mt Sir Sandford (11,590 ft/3533 m) in the Selkirks but excellent climbing on rock, snow and ice is found throughout these ranges and that on the granite spires of the Purcell's Bugaboo group is world renowned.

The Coast Mountains rise from the deeply indented Pacific shore and, except in the vicinity of Vancouver, are virtually expeditionary mountains to which sea-planes are the best means of approach. Poor weather, extensive glaciers but splendid mountains characterise the range. The highest summits lie towards the south where magnificent Mt Waddington (13,177 ft/4016 m) dominates a region of ice-hung granite aiguilles reminiscent of the Mt Blanc Range. The northern section, spilling over into the Alaska panhandle, also contains some impressive but rather lower peaks including the graceful ice pyramid of Kate's Needle (10,023 ft/3055 m) and the striking Devil's Thumb (9077 ft/2767 m) rock tower.

A vast knot of mountains rise where British Columbia, the Yukon and Alaska meet. These are the St Elias Mountains where two giants of

Himalayan proportions—Mt St Elias (18,008 ft/5489 m) and Mt Logan (19,520 ft/5950 m)—stand among hundreds of icy peaks above the largest glaciers outside the polar regions. Great mountaineering routes have been made here but all access is expeditionary, aircraft are commonly used, and incessant bad weather renders climbing extremely committing and failure is commonplace. Climbing in the small and beautiful Fairweather Range—a southern offshoot—(Mt Fairweather—15,318 ft/4669 m) is further threatened by occasional serious earthquakes.

Mountaineering in Alaska is now well developed and its fine peaks—many of international significance—are a popular goal for American and foreign mountaineers. Here too an expeditionary commitment is essential for, although actual ascents are now often attempted in alpine style, it is only the free use of aircraft that has allowed any reasonable access to these usually remote mountains with their arctic weather. Although worthy climbs are made in the coastal Chugach Range (Mt Marcus Baker—13,176 ft/4016 m) and the more gentle Wrangells (Mt Blackburn—16,390 ft/4996 m) and the extensive Brooks Range of the far north is being opened (Mt Isto—9060 ft/2761 m), it is the 400 mile (650 km) arc of the Alaska Range that is the major attraction. The icy colossus of Mt McKinley (20,322 ft/6194 m) dwarfs all other peaks of the range, relatively few of which actually exceed 10,000 feet (3000 m) in height. The easiest of the several routes on this, the highest summit in North America, is of no technical difficulty but formidable weather and high altitude ensure that this much frequented climb is a serious undertaking. Typically the other important peaks are sharp-ridged ice-peaks rising steeply above large glaciers. They include the fluted ice-pyramid of Mt Huntington (12,240 ft/3731 m)—perhaps America's most beautiful mountain—savage Mt Deborah (12,540 ft/3822 m) and the spectacular Kichatna Spires, reminiscent of Patagonia, which rise almost to 9000 feet (2740 m).

South America

The narrow chain of the Andes stretches some 5000 miles (8000 km) from the warm Caribbean to Cape Horn only 2400 miles (3900 km) from the South Pole. It crosses many different climatic zones and embraces high deserts and soaring rock needles, the world's largest area of equatorial ice and three distinct regions of active volcanoes. In many places the mountains rise over the ruins of past civilisations. The few mountains outside the Andes are of little importance. Big-wall style climbs have been made on the great mesas of the Guiana Highlands where Roraima rises from tropical rain forest to 9219 feet (2810 m), and on the granite domes of the Serra do Mar outside Rio de Janeiro, but the mountain spine lies on the other side of the continent.

The Andes' northernmost group is Colombia's isolated Sierra Nevada de Santa Marta, a compact area of beautiful valleys and small lakes dominated by the twin glacier-clad peaks of Cristobel Colon and Simon Bolivar which rise to 18,947 feet (5775 m) just 30 miles (50 km) from the sea. There is some good rock-climbing here on sound granite. Eastwards in Venezuela the small rock and ice peaks of the Sierra Nevada de Marida reach 16,410 feet (5002 m) on Pico Bolivar. These are popular mountains easily accessible from Lake Maracaibo only 40 miles (65 km) distant. Although the Andes cross Colombia as three distinct crests, the only other mountains of real interest are the heavily glaciated Sierra Nevada de Cocuy north of Bogota. There are large rock faces but the group is notorious for mists and bad weather and little other than ordinary ascents has been accomplished. Ecuador however claims perhaps the finest series of volcanoes in the world, more than a dozen top 17,000 feet (5180 m) and the highest—Chimborazo (20,561 ft/6267 m)—was once considered the world's highest mountain! Its ascent and that of other ice-hung volcanoes such as Cotapaxi (19,347 ft/5897 m)—famed for its classic beauty—are largely straightforward snow climbs although more difficult routes on rock and ice have been made recently.

Best known of the Andes are those of Peru. Typically they are splendid ice peaks, their ridges crusted with wild ice formations and their fluted faces rising from tortured glaciers. Arid moorlands and little lakes lie beneath the peaks. Claimed by some as the world's most beautiful mountains, they are certainly popular for the weather is settled, approaches are short while the climbing—largely on ice or mixed ground—is of all standards. Virtually all summits have been climbed and modern guide-books cover the major ranges. Trekking has recently become popular.

The Cordillera Blanca is the most extensive range where 70 summits reach above 18,000 feet (5480 m), 11 of them topping 20,000 feet (6100 m). Huascaran (22,208 ft/6769 m) is the highest peak while handsome Yerupaja (21,759 ft/6632 m) stands in the adjoining but smaller Cordillera Huayash. The lesser ranges of the south-east, the Vilcabamba, the Vilcanota and the Apolobamba, are more alpine in character although the former is dominated by Salcantay (20,574 ft/6271 m) and formidable Pumasillo (19,915 ft/6070 m). The line is continued into Bolivia by the generally similar Cordillera Real although the climate is drier and the snowline higher. Illimani (21,277 ft/6485 m) close to La Paz, is the highest peak.

A line of barren volcanoes, several over 21,000 feet (6400 m), stretch through the Atacama region from south-western Peru through Bolivia and into Chile to form the Argentinian march. Here stands dormant Ojos del Salado (22,539 ft/6870 m)—the world's highest volcano. Indian remains have recently been discovered on summits as high as 22,057 foot (6723 m) Llullaillaco.

Fine mountaineering is again found in the mountains of central Chile, together with some first class skiing. Access from Santiago is easy and such summits as Marmolejo (20,013 ft/6100 m) and Cerro Plomo (17,815 ft/5430 m) are justifiably popular. There are difficult technical climbs on rock, snow and ice. This region of the Andes is dominated however by the hemisphere's highest peak—mighty Aconcagua—which stands on the Argentine side of the border 70 miles (110 km) west of the alpine resort of Mendoza. The mountain is much frequented, there are two high huts and the ascent is a straightforward plod: but Aconcagua possesses the characteristics of a fair sized Himalayan peak with even worse weather and few parties actually reach the summit. Noteworthy among the more interesting of the mountain's routes is the stupendous 10,000 foot (3000 m) South Face. Five hundred miles (800 km) to the south lies the beautiful Andean Lakes District. Difficult rock routes have been made here among such impressive alpine peaks as Tronador (11,253 ft/3430 m) and Cerro Tres Picos (8530 ft/2600 m).

Beyond latitude 42° lies Patagonia—the final thousand miles of the continent. Dramatic ice-glazed rock spires and two large ice-caps separate the wild storm-lashed fjords and forests of the west coast from the flat and arid pampas of the east. Jutting from the northern ice-cap, San Valentin (13,204 ft/4025 m) is Patagonia's highest summit but the most important mountains are those of the Fitzroy and Paine groups rising respectively from the eastern and southern flanks of the larger southern ice-cap which is fully 250 miles (400 km) in length. Fitzroy itself (11,073 ft/3375 m) is a striking rock aiguille while attempts on the impossible-looking spire of Cerro Torre (10,280 ft/3133 m) have generated much controversy. The fang of Paine Grande rises to 10,600 feet (3230 m) and while both groups are famous for big-wall type climbs of great severity, they are notorious for the worst weather in the world. Daunting weather is also a characteristic of the lovely but mysterious mountains of Tierra del Fuego which rise, ice encrusted and mist enshrouded, above glaciers which flow into the sea. Mount Darwin (8110 ft/2472 m) is the final high peak of the continent.

The Polar Regions
With an average elevation of over 6000 feet (1900 m) the Antarctic is the world's highest continent. From its vast ice-cap protrude several moun-

tain ranges, their peaks usually smaller than their altitude might suggest, the loftiest of which are the strangely sharp and angular mountains of the Sentinel Range which rise to 16,860 feet (5139 m). Other mountains are exposed on the coasts, notably on the Antarctic Peninsula and its adjacent islands where splendid peaks, reminiscent of the Alps but mostly below 9000 feet (2700 m), rise amid magnificent glacier and fjord scenery. Most of the many ascents made on the continent have been for scientific purposes and access otherwise is so difficult and expensive as to be impractical.

Any mountaineering challenge offered by such tiny sub-Antarctic sea-mounts as Kerguelen, Bouvet and Heard is minimised by the perpetual blizzards that sweep the Southern Ocean, and the only attractive island is the largest, South Georgia. Here is a permanent settlement and several expeditions have climbed among the sharp and heavily glaciated peaks which rise to 9000 feet (2700 m).

Greenland's magnificent mountains ring the edge of the vast ice-cap which covers most of this great island and rises centrally to 10,000 feet (3050 m). Gunnbjorn's Fjeld (12,139 ft/3700 m) in the Watkins Mountains of the east coast is the highest summit, but most peaks, typically rocky aiguilles, are considerably lower. Mountaineering here is expeditionary and approaches, by boat, ski or plane, are often difficult especially on the east coast where sea-ice may disrupt travel during the short summer season. Relatively stable weather and regular flights from Europe to the major settlements have, nevertheless, made Greenland a popular goal for small expeditions. The Staunings Alps on the east coast, where some 70 granite peaks of alpine scale surround Dansketinde (9613 ft/2960 m), is the most developed region and is even guidebooked.

A tangle of mountains and several sizable ice-caps form the backbone of Baffin Island. Thanks to a regular air service a number of small expeditions have operated here, mostly in the region of the Pangnirtung Pass on the Cumberland Peninsula. Several big-wall climbs have been made on the truly spectacular prows and spires of ice-carved granite that line this deep defile. Close by, Mount Asgard (6598 ft/2011 m)—a pair of huge flat-topped pillars—must be one of the world's most unusual peaks although it is not the highest summit. Baffin's other mountains are little known.

Africa
Africa is the least mountainous of the continents and it holds least permanent ice: the three small areas of glacier that linger do so—enigmatically—astride the Equator. Yet Africa presents unlimited scope to the rock-climber and splendid unique mountains to the mountaineer.

Behind the coasts of Algeria and Morocco the Atlas extend for 1300 miles (2100 km) rarely rising above 7000 feet (2100 m) before rearing in the far west as the High Atlas where some 250 miles (400 km) of jagged ridges and deep valleys contain a dozen summits of over 12,000 feet (3960 m). White in winter under heavy snow, or in summer harsh and arid, the High Atlas is the frontier between the scorching Sahara and the benign ocean littoral. Although access from Europe is today easy, only the Toubkal group, where rise the highest summits, is much frequented. (Toubkal itself : 13,665 ft/4165 m.) The peaks are typically massive rather than elegant, often with wide tops from which fall steep rocky faces and tangled buttresses. All the major summits are easily gained but there is good rock-climbing—often on granite—and several fine ridge traverses besides interesting ski-mountaineering. Winter snow climbing and spring trekking are becoming popular, there are several climbing huts and a well-developed ski resort located at Oukaimeden.

A thousand miles (1600 km) south-eastward and just within Algeria an isolated cluster of spectacular rock needles rise from the desert—the Hoggar. The best known, although not the highest, is the magnificent aiguille of Ilamane (9050 ft/2758 m) and the many expeditions that have visited the range since 1935 have enjoyed steep and sensational climbing on the good basaltic rock of this and other peaks. In Chad, 700 miles (1100 km) to the east, stand the seven massifs of Tibesti. The highest is Emi Koussi (11,204 ft/3415 m). Although visually exciting, the volcanic rock is poor and several expeditions have discovered little of mountaineering interest to repay their arduous journey.

Politically turbulent and still enjoying an aura of mystery, Ethiopia is almost entirely mountainous. The highest of the nine major groups is the extraordinary Simien where Ras Dashan rises to 15,159 feet (4620 m). While most summits are accessible by mule, the terrain is wild and a profusion of huge basalt cliffs and isolated pinnacles await the cragsman. Virtually no serious mountaineering has been attempted.

Usually shrouded in mist, the legendary 'Mountains of the Moon'— the Ruwenzori—stand on the Uganda/Zaire frontier just 20 miles (32 km) north of the Equator (Plates 12, 34, 58). Six of the eleven major massifs hold small glaciers and ten of the summits, characteristically plastered with peculiar ice formations, top 16,000 feet (4875 m). The highest is elegant Margherita (16,763 ft/5109 m) above the Stanley Massif. The higher peaks have been well explored with all the more obvious lines ascended and the best climbs are in alpine style on mixed ground or ice and have a unique flavour. Below the peaks beautiful tarns lie in craggy valleys draped in the weird and dense vegetation for which the Range is noted. A series of climbing huts are in ruins but there are many excellent caves and so, politics allowing, access to these exciting mountains is only semi-expeditionary. But beware! The Ruwenzori bogs are notorious!

Isolated Mount Kenya is world famous—its twin rocky fangs just clearing 17,000 feet (5180 m), hung with no less than 15 tiny glaciers and surrounded by its cluster of satellite spires (Plates 33, 53). It is Africa's most alpine mountain and compares well to the best of the Chamonix Aiguilles. The two principal summits can be reached only by serious technical climbing while excellent rock and steep ice provide a series of splendid routes, many of great character and extreme difficulty. Nine climbing huts ring the mountain and the surrounding high moorlands, dotted with little green tarns, give superb if strenuous hiking. Access is easy enough for already acclimatised Nairobi alpinists to snatch major climbs at weekends and the mountain is deservedly popular.

The aloof and ice-draped cone of massive Kilimanjaro is a familiar safari backdrop (Plate 32). The highest mountain in Africa, it is a dormant volcano and its principal summit, Kibo (19,340 ft/5895 m) contains a huge ice-choked crater from which glacier tongues cascade down its flanks. By its easiest route, and aided by a series of modern mountain huts, its ascent is a straightforward multi-day hike and extremely popular. But Kibo's awesome south-western flank is remote and rarely frequented and 4000 foot (1200 m) cliffs and tumbling ice-falls provide magnificent mountaineering of a most serious nature and almost Himalayan style. Eight miles (13 km) eastward the pinnacled ridge of Mawenzi (16,890 ft/5148 m)—the rocky secondary summit—gives noteworthy climbing but on poor rock while an ascent of its stupendous East Face is a major undertaking. Now within a Tanzanian National Park, access to Kilimanjaro is carefully controlled.

Mountainous country rims much of the plateau that is southern Africa. In Malawi the Mlanje massif (9843 ft/3000 m) is the culminating point of an enchanting region of high moorlands, craggy summits and large rock faces where several long and difficult climbs of high quality have been made. In Zimbabwe the Chimanimani rise over 8500 feet (2600 m) and have been likened to the Scottish Highlands. They have been well developed by local climbers. Westward in Namibia, however, the several chains of arid and craggy mountains of similar height are but little known although they contain some impressive rock peaks.

Climbing is a popular and well developed pastime in South Africa and hundreds of beautiful and shapely peaks form a broken chain of some 1200 miles (1900 km) behind the eastern and southern coasts. Highest are the spectacular Drakensberg where several summits clear 10,000

feet (3000 m) and Thabana Ntlenyana (11,425 ft/3482 m)—in Lesotho—
is the highest summit south of Kilimanjaro. Basalt faces and proud
pinnacles offer climbing but on poor rock. Among the ranges of the
south west, the Cedarberg and the Hex River Range are justly famed for
the excellent climbs on their large sandstone and quartzite cliffs. In
winter there are considerable snow falls and winter climbing and skiing
are possible. Finally there is Table Mountain, rising to only 3566 feet
(1087 m) from the suburbs of Cape Town, insulted with a cable railway,
and yet its crags laced with over 500 difficult rock-climbs. Is it perhaps
the most climbed on single mountain in the world?

But these are only Africa's important mountains. The great Rift
Valleys are studded with active and dormant volcanoes, those of
Virunga rising to 14,783 feet (4506 m) and Mount Cameroon, the only
big mountain in West Africa, reaching 13,350 feet (4069 m). Such
mountains offer impressive hikes! Elsewhere there is rock aplenty, not
only in gorges and outcrops but on the isolated inselbergs and cliff-girt
mesas that are often a feature of the African landscape. It is safe to
assume that African climbing will be unusual!

Australasia and the Pacific
Pride of place in an area which covers over one third of the globe must
go to the noble mountains of New Zealand, where some of the finest
alpine peaks in the world rise from the 500 mile (800 km) mountainous
spine of the South Island. Mount Cook (12,349 ft/3764 m) dominates a
spectacular region where dozens of summits top 10,000 feet (3000 m)
and which, but for its less reliable rock, compares favourably with
Europe's Mont Blanc Range. The Southern Alps are characterised by
the heaviest temperate-zone glaciation outside the Himalaya and mountaineering—with ice and mixed climbing as a speciality—and skiing
are well developed and popular. Access to the Mount Cook National Park
is easy. Other mountain groups to north and south are no less interesting, especially the Haast Range around Matterhorn-like Mount Aspiring
(9959 ft/3036 m), but often poor weather and thick forests make
approaches difficult. Several graceful volcanoes, among them Mount
Egmont (8260 ft/2518 m), rise in the North Island and offer noteworthy
skiing.

Australia is barren and almost flat by comparison and its mountains
have been worn to mere stumps by the ravages of time. Mount Kosci-
usko, the continent's highest point, rises from the largely forest-clad
Great Dividing Range which parallels the east coast and reaches only
7328 feet (2234 m). There is no permanent snow, although in winter the
surrounding Snowy Mountains (5000 ft/1500 m) provide good skiing.

Wilderness tramping—or 'bush-whacking'—is a local sport while technical climbing of an extremely high standard has been developed on the abundance of steep rock, often close to the big cities. In the arid interior rise strange rock formations such as the famous Ayers Rock (2845 ft/867 m) which, with other features, have attracted climbers. Tasmania however does contain real mountains whose craggy summits, guarded by fierce bush and poor weather, rise to around 5000 feet (1500 m). The long and difficult routes on excellent rock which have been made here are the nearest thing to alpine climbs in Australia. Sea-cliffs too provide good sport and especially interesting is Ball's Pyramid in the Tasman Sea, probably the world's highest sea-stack, whose 1843 foot (562 m) summit has now been reached by several hard routes.

New Guinea contains the world's third area of equatorial ice. The entire spine of this large island is mountainous and, despite thick jungles, tangled foothills and political problems, several expeditions have climbed here in recent years, notably in the vicinity of Carstenz Pyramid (16,532 ft/5039 m). This peak is the island's highest point and rises in West Irian. Retreating glaciers and huge limestone walls are a feature of the region and excellent mountaineering has been reported. Eastward in Papuan territory the Bismark Range rises to nearly 15,000 feet (4600 m) and the Owen Stanley Range to above 13,000 feet (3950 m). Doubtless there is some potential among these little explored mountains?

Although all the Indonesian islands are mountainous, the high volcanoes that rise above the tree-line are of little interest to mountaineers. This is usually the case elsewhere in Southeast Asia, for although several summits reach 10,000 feet (3000 m) the jungle reaches as high. A notable exception however is the granite massif of Kinabalu (13,455 ft/4100 m) in the Malaysian state of Sabah on the island of Borneo. Tremendous cliffs of 3000 feet (900 m) or more fall from a wide and pinnacled summit plateau and several long and worthwhile climbs have been made. Access is restricted by thick jungle although one straightforward route, with two huts, is easily approached.

There is scope for climbing on the extremely rugged island of Taiwan which rises to over 13,000 feet (3900 m) and holds great crags, deep gorges and high sea-cliffs. Its highest point, Yu Shan, is an easy scramble. Several groups of very attractive small mountains grace the gnarled Korean peninsula, the most interesting being the Taebaek Range which reach around 5000 feet (1500 m) astride the DMZ near the east coast. Here there is fine hiking while imposing granite spires and crags offer good rock-climbing. Quite a lot of climbing has also been done on little rock peaks and granite domes in the vicinity of Seoul, the capital.

Japan is a major mountaineering nation and, as one might expect, climbing on the mountains which rise from all four of her main islands is well developed and is today a most popular mass sport. Most interest is centred on the Japanese Alps where sixteen summits top 10,000 feet (3050 m), the highest of which is Kitadake (10,472 ft/3192 m). Typically high and sharp ridges link successions of rugged and angular peaks, most of them of granite. The weather is markedly seasonal and heavy winter snows linger in patches well into summer. Beautiful forests of great variety clothe the lower slopes. Access from the cities is easy and many climbing huts are scattered throughout the three main alpine groups, all of which lie within a radius of 130 miles (210 km) from Tokyo. The northern group is the most frequented. Japan's highest summit however is the classic volcanic cone of Fuji-san (12,388 ft/ 3776 m). While its beauty is world renowned it is not a mountaineer's peak for its ascent is an easy and crowded hike and it is just one of some sixty volcanoes scattered throughout the Japanese islands.

Asia and the Himalaya

The Pamir Knot, situated at approximately longitude 75°E latitude 37°N —somehwere between the Whakhan and the Taghdumbash Pamir—is the hub of Asia and from it the great ranges fan out like spokes of a wheel. First west and then south-west stretches the chain of the Hindu Kush, walling Pakistan from Afghanistan and the Turkestan deserts. An arid range where big mountains hung with large glaciers rise above bare and dusty hills, the parched valleys are green only where irrigation has allowed cultivation to surround the villages. Chief of the twenty summits that exceed 23,000 feet (7000 m) and typically fairly straightforward to climb, is the great mass of Tirich Mir (25,263 ft/7700 m), but lower peaks of around 20,000 feet (7000 m) to the south-west have provided challenging alpine-style climbs to very small parties. Southward across the deep Chitral valley springs the Hindu Raj and the linked Trans-Indus ranges of Swat and Kohistan. This is a greener and more beautiful region with several formidable peaks, highest of which is Koyo Zom (22,603 ft/6889 m).

The mountain line extends through Iran and into Turkey. Although the dormant snow-covered volcano of Demavend (18,603 ft/5670 m)—a popular scramble easily accessible from Tehran—is Iran's highest point, it is the Takht-i-Suleiman, or 'Solomon's Throne' massif, which is of mountaineering interest. Several expeditions have found fine climbing here especially on Alam Kuh (15,880 ft/4840 m) which boasts a formidable 200 foot (600 m) face and several small glaciers. Ararat (16,945 ft/ 5165 m) is Turkey's highest summit, its isolated glacier-hung volcanic cone rearing over both Turkish and Soviet Armenia and giving a straightforward three day climb. Southward the beautiful Hakkari Mountains of Turkish Kurdistan culminate in the massifs of Cilo Dag (13,681 ft/4170 m) and Sat Dag (12,500 ft/3810 m) where spiky rock peaks cradle small glaciers and offer rewarding sport. Other interesting Turkish mountains are the lush Pontines above the Black Sea coast and the Taurus of the Mediterranean littoral, both with difficult rock peaks exceeding 12,000 feet (3700 m), while there are good limestone crags on the south-west coast near Antalya.

Directly north of the Pamir Knot is the Pamir Range itself, a mass of high ground some 200 miles (350 km) square lying largely in Soviet Turkestan from the heart of which rises the Oxus River. A series of roughly parallel mountain crests rise above broad bleak valleys—or 'pamirs'—and give birth to huge glaciers before rising to typically massive icy peaks. Notable summits include the Soviet Union's highest —Pik Communism (24,551 ft/7483 m) which remarkably for such altitude boasts more than 15 different routes—and Pik Lenin (23,406 ft/ 7134 m) the most frequented big mountain in the world. Great traverses over many tops, a Soviet speciality, are among the hard and committing climbs that have been made here. Approaches are often difficult and visits by western mountaineers, as to other Soviet mountains, are possible but under restrictive conditions. The contiguous Kashgar Range of Chinese Turkestan is virtually unknown to recent western climbers but holds the very highest Pamir summits, Qungur II (25,325 ft/ 7719 m) and Muztagh Ata (24,758 ft/7546 m) which rise from two conspicuous massifs above a more verdant area.

Running north-east from the Pamirs is the thousand mile (1600 km) crest of the Tien Shan or 'Celestial Mountains', the northern wall of the great desert basin of Takla Makan. Initially lining the Sino-Soviet frontier, the range rises to a group of massive peaks and huge glaciers before plunging deep into Sinkiang to fade away against the distant Mongolian border. These great peaks are extremely remote: Pik Pobeda (24,407 ft/7439 m) is the Soviet Union's second summit yet it was not located until 1946. Some fine climbs have been made recently in this savage yet beautiful region. Lesser but more alpine peaks lie westwards and are easily accessible from the cities of Alma Ata and Frunze.

South-east from the Pamirs stretches the Kun Lun Shan, among the more mysterious of Central Asia's myriad mountains, forming the southern wall of the Takla Makan and dividing Sinkiang from Tibet itself. The highest summit is probably Ulugh Mustagh (c.25,350 ft/7727 m) but there appear to be many tops exceeding 22,000 feet (6700 m). After a thousand miles the mountains sweep down into south-western China where Minya Konka (24,892 ft/7587 m) and Amne Machin

(23,490 ft/7160 m) are notable peaks.

The Karakorum rise south-east below the Pamir Knot largely in Pakistan—a complex range some 250 miles (400 km) in length containing some of the most magnificent mountains on earth. Typically great angular ice peaks or savage rock fangs, they are impressive rather than beautiful and stand in avenues beside huge glaciers from which pour thunderous rivers to join the Indus or the doomed Yarkand. The region is arid, a desert virtually beyond reach of the monsoon and only a high winter snow fall and constant irrigation make possible the green oasis, lush with barley, apricot groves and poplar trees, so characteristic of its valleys. Nineteen peaks tower above 25,000 feet (7600 m) while no less than six of the summits clustering round the head of the Baltoro Glacier exceed 26,000 feet (7925 m)—among them K2, the world's second highest mountain (28,253 ft/8612 m), Broad Peak, Hidden Peak and the Gasherbrums. Other famous peaks that line the Baltoro include Masherbrum and the Mustagh and Trango Towers while the Ogre and Kunyang Kish flank the 60 mile (100 km) Hispar-Biafo Glacier system with Rakaposhi and Haramosh rising to the south-west. Karakorum approach marches are usually long and arduous and logistic problems often severe, yet much climbing is done in the range by mountaineers of many nations. All the higher summits have now been reached and today the accent is on small parties, climbing ideally in alpine style, forcing new routes or making technically challenging first ascents of the myriad small peaks. Spectacular if strenuous trekking up the great glaciers is a recent development.

The Himalaya—the Ultimate Mountains: for over 1500 miles (2400 km) this mantle of mighty peaks sweeps round the shoulders of the Indian sub-continent. This crystal wall, the greatest on earth, guards the teeming plains, the lush valleys and the ancient cultures of India, Nepal and Bhutan from the arid and empty plateaux of the World's Roof—from Tibet and China. Drained, and contained, entirely by three great rivers—the Indus, the Tsangpo or Brahmaputra, and the Ganges— these are sacred mountains to both Hindu and Buddhist.

Nanga Parbat (26,660 ft/8125 m) is the far western bastion of the Himalaya. A huge isolated ice-hung massif of compelling grandeur, it stands 150 miles (240 km) south of the Pamir Knot and over 23,000 feet (7000 m) above the desolate gorges of the Indus curling round its feet. It is one of the world's great mountains with an aura of strange malevolence which echoes its history. Traditionally this far western end of the Himalaya lies in Kashmir but because of the Kashmir Dispute Nanga Parbat today stands in Pakistan while eastward over the cease-fire line the 300 mile (500 km) block of the Punjab Himalaya stands in India.

Highest of the Punjab summits is shapely Nun Kun (23,410 ft/7135 m) but most are considerably lower. It is country ideally suited to small expeditions climbing in alpine style and the jagged peaks of Kishtwar, verdent Kulu and arid Zaskar offer superb climbing and even good ski-mountaineering.

Abode of many Hindu deities, the lovely mountains of Garhwal cradle the infant Ganges and stretch from Sutlej to the Nepalese border. Access is easy and Garwhal was explored early, being compared to a scaled-up Switzerland with its splendid forests and flower-filled meadows. Nanda Devi (25,645 ft/7817 m) is the giant of the region and rises above its famous 'Sanctuary' surrounded by nineteen peaks topping 21,000 feet (6400 m) including the white granite tooth of Changabang. Other important peaks are Kamet (25,447 ft/7756 m)—the world's first 25,000 foot summit to be climbed back in 1931—and formidable Shivling (21,467 ft/ 6543 m)—the 'Matterhorn of Garhwal'. Dozens of fine mountains rise above 20,000 feet (6000 m).

The green, fruitful and well-populated kingdom of Nepal was first opened to foreigners only in 1949 and the government's continuing policy of restricting access to certain areas—besides long and difficult communications—have ensured that remote West Nepal remains relatively unknown. The major summits have, nevertheless, all been climbed. The icy chisel-shaped peaks of Api and Nampa rise respectively to 23,399 feet (7132 m) and 22,162 feet (6755 m) in the far north-western corner. The tangled ridges of the Kanjiroba Himal (22,580 ft/6882 m) are guarded by profound and difficult gorges while the long crest of the Dhaula Himal, with 15 formidable summits over 'Seven-thousand-metres' (23,000 ft) is well explored. At its eastern end stands the huge wind-blasted triangle of Dhaulagiri I (26,795 ft/8167 m)—one of the world's great mountains, its 9th highest.

The summits of Dhaulagiri I and Annapurna I (26,545 ft/8091 m) are separated by a distance of only 21 miles (34 km)—and the 23,000 feet (7000 m) gorge of the Kali Gandaki, the world's deepest. An icy rampart some 30 miles (50 km) long, the Annapurna Himal, has 11 summits rising above 'Seven-thousand-metres' and a score of fine lesser tops including noble Machapuchare (22,958 ft/6997 m)—the 'Fish's Tail' (Plate 7). The Gurkha Himal contain the proud and important peaks of Manaslu (26,760 ft/8156 m), Himalchuli (25,896 ft/7893 m) (Plate 36) and Peak 29, while the Ganesh Himal (Ganesh I—24,298 ft/7406 m), well seen from Kathmandu, is a group of daunting ice peaks several of which are, at the time of writing, still virgin. Central Nepal, from the Kali Gandaki eastward to Everest, is the most popular region of the Himalaya for trekking and offers itineraries both long and short, high and low.

Now the Langtang and adjoining Jugal Himals line the Tibetan frontier and contain a host of superb icy summits up to 23,000 feet (7000 m), many still unclimbed. Standing just north is long and craggy Shisha Pangma or Gosainthan (26,398 ft/8046 m)—China's (Tibet's) highest summit. The remote glen of Rolwaling, guarded by formidable double-headed Gaurishankar (23,440 ft/7146 m), leads over a high pass to the Mahalungar or Khumbu Himal. This is the beautiful home country of the sherpas where white peaks soar above neat villages and high open pastures. Here rise many famous mountains including three of the world's eight highest—Everest (29,028 ft/8848 m) (Plates 38, 68, 69), Lhotse (27,923 ft/8511 m) (Plate 70) and Cho Oyu (26,750 ft/8153 m)— besides lower and more spectacular peaks such as fang-like Ama Dablam (Plates 3, 37). East of Everest are the wild and unfrequented valleys of Hongu and the Khumbakarna Himal dominated by the handsome pyramid of Makalu (27,825 ft/8481 m)—the world's fifth highest mountain. Much here is still officially virgin.

The high crest of the Kangchenjunga massif divides Nepal from Sikkim. Kangchenjunga itself is the world's third highest mountain (28,208 ft/8595 m) and with its massed satellites, of which Jannu (25,294 ft/7710 m) is the best known, form the 'Five Treasuries of the Great Snows' —the famous panorama seen from the Indian hill station of Darjeeling. Both far eastern Nepal and Sikkim are politically sensitive areas and much climbing still remains to be done. Strongly influenced by the monsoon, the lush forested landscape of the Himalaya's final 500 miles (800 km) holds many 'Seven-thousand-metre' peaks and several enormous glaciers but the Kingdom of Bhutan and the Indian state of Assam are little known, for access is either restricted or forbidden. Suffice to say that the beautiful white cone of Namche Barwa (25,445 ft/7756 m)— towering 18,000 feet (5500 m) above the Tsangpo Gorge looped around its foot—is a fitting final bastion to the greatest range on earth. A range where all the major summits have now been climbed, and the stage set for some 'real' mountaineering on the hundreds of peaks that remain inviolate.

The Eiger

3
Ten Great Mountains

The Eiger (13,036 ft/3970 m)
Bernese Alps, Switzerland (Plate 6)

The Eiger has always had a malevolent reputation—its very name, the Ogre, bears witness to that. It sits hunched and brooding over the alpine meadows of Kleine Scheidegg, its north face dark and ugly and seemingly impregnable with one icefield atop another and steep limestone rock-bands in between. The battle to climb this North Face in the thirties with its heavy toll of life and its coincidence with the height of Nazi fervour only served to compound the mountain's notoriety.

The Eiger summit was first trodden in 1858 by Charles Barrington with Christian Almer and Peter Bohren; the Southwest Ridge was climbed in 1874 and the South Ridge in 1876. The long Mittellegi Ridge, dropping to the northeast, resisted attempts for a long time—it was descended with the aid of rappels by Grindelwald guides in 1885 but it was not until 1921 that it was climbed by three guides with a young Japanese alpinist. In 1932 the Northeast Face was climbed by Hans Lauper, A. Zurchner, J. Knubel and A. Graven, and then top climbers began to look at the fearsome North Face—the North Faces of the Matterhorn and Jorasses had just been climbed, and the 'Eigerwand' was now the most coveted prize. The face, a crucible for sudden storms, has a structure that demanded a zig-zag route, making retreat very difficult. The first eight men to attempt the face all died. It was easy to see how the word *Nordwand* (North Face) came to be translated into *Mordwand* (Killer Face) in the public mind, particularly after the tragedy of 1936 in which four more climbers died, the last, Kurz, being left for a long time alive, dangling on a rope, while desperate rescue attempts were made. He finally succumbed, his rescuers only a few feet away. Even then, they couldn't reach his body and it hung grimly on the face until another party was able to cut it down.

Later contenders managed to retreat safely and the face was finally climbed in 1938 by Anderl Heckmair, Heinrich Harrer, Ludwig Vorg and Fritz Kasparek. After World War 2 climbers of all nationalities came to attempt the climb and the route was repeated regularly. There were still fatalities but the mountain gradually began to lose some of its sinister reputation. In 1961 the first winter ascent was made; the first British ascent was by Chris Bonington and Ian Clough in 1962; the first solo climb by Michel Darbelley in 1963; then in 1966 a new Direct route was attempted in winter. Two teams, initially in competition, battled for the straight-up line in a blaze of press publicity. John Harlin, American leader of one of the groups, was killed when a fixed rope broke below the 'White Spider'; the two teams then united and the route was completed by Dougal Haston and four German climbers.

In 1968 a Polish route was opened up, crossing the North Pillar and finishing up the Lauper Route, whilst simultaneously a new route, crossing the Polish Route, was set up on the North Pillar by a party including the brothers Reinhold and Gunther Messner. In 1969 Japanese climbers forced a route up the righthand side of the face, using vast quantities of equipment and taking several weeks to complete. The fastest time up the Eigerwand was made by Reinhold Messner and Peter Habeler in 1973 in 10 hours by the now classic Heckmair Route.

Grandes Jorasses (13,799 ft/4208 m)
Mont Blanc Massif
Franco-Italian border

Tucked in the heart of the Mont Blanc range is the Grandes Jorasses; its North Face towering over the Leschaux Glacier is one of the most imposing sights in the Alps. It is as if six mountains had been sandwiched together to produce one great granite facade, buttressed by a series of parallel spurs. The highest of the six summits is the most easterly, the Pointe Walker, and the summit ridge continues westwards with the Pointes Whymper, Croz, Hélène, Marguerite and Young. The southern face is much more broken and provides easier access; this was the way the first climbers came. Edward Whymper was the first to reach one of the summits the second highest in 1865, a few weeks before his famous ascent of the Matterhorn. The higher summit was climbed three years later by Hubert Walker with his guides M. Anderegg, J. Jaun and J. Grange, initially following a similar route to Whymper from Courmayeur, then traversing right to reach the summit of the Pointe Walker. This is now known as the Ordinary Route.

It was another 41 years before all the summits on the ridge had been climbed and attention turned towards the steep ridge that drops abruptly from the Pointe Walker to the Col des Hirondelles, the Hiron-

Grandes Jorasses

delles or North East Ridge. In 1911 Geoffrey Winthrop Young and H.O. Jones, with their guides Joseph Knubel and Laurent Croux, traversed the complete summit crest of the mountain and descended the Hirondelles Ridge, but although there followed several attempts to climb up it, it resisted until 1927 when it was eventually surmounted by a group of Italians.

A crucial development now took place. All over the Alps a new generation of climbers began looking to the steep and intimidating faces between the ridges. In 1931 the Matterhorn North Wall was climbed, and it was the turn next of the Grandes Jorasses. Several attempts were made on its North Face by different routes and the mountain claimed several victims before Rudolf Peters and Martin Maier succeeded in climbing the North Spur of the Point Croz in 1935. Though it is not the longest spur to the highest summit—that is the Walker Spur—attention switched for a time to the Eigerwand and only when that had been climbed in 1938, were renewed attempts made on the Jorasses. Lecco climber, Riccardo Cassin, took up the challenge; he had been too late for the Eiger and was determined to snatch the 'Walker', the current 'last great problem' in the Alps. With Ugo Tizzoni and Gino Esposito he succeeded in 1938 in climbing what is surely one of the most beautiful routes in the Alps. It took three days, and for steepness, length and difficulty outstripped the earlier Croz route. The first winter ascent of the Walker Spur was made by W. Bonatti and C. Zapelli in 1964 and the first solo ascent by A. Gogna in 1968. For several years climbers had been attracted by a very formidable looking 3000 foot (900 m) ice field, the Shroud, to the left of the Walker Spur, and steeper than 65° in places. It was finally forced by R. Desmaison and R. Flematty in the winter of 1968 after they had discounted a previous claim by an unknown solo climber. Attempting another new route between the Shroud and the Walker in the winter of 1971, Desmaison's companion died in a blizzard and Desmaison himself was winched to safety after 15 days.

Mount Kenya (17,058 ft/5199 m)
Kenya (Plates 2, 33, 53)

Mount Kenya—or Kere-Nyaga in Kikuyu, Mountain of Brightness—rises, a twin-headed fang inlaid with glaciers, 12,000 feet (3500 m) above the Kenya plateau, only ten miles south of the Equator. In splendid

Mount Kenya

isolation it floats above the hot savannah, often visible from as far as 100 miles away. The peak is the eroded plug of an ancient volcano, its rock nepheline-syenite, a coarse-textured rock resembling granite. The twin summits of Batian (17,058 ft/5199 m) and Nelion (17,022 ft/5188 m) are separated by the icy gash known as the Gate of Mists and surrounded by a cluster of satellite aiguilles cradling no fewer than 15 small glaciers. Because of its equatorial position, the southern side of the mountain has a summer season in January and February, whilst the northern side is 'in condition' during August and September. The opposite flank meanwhile is plastered in snow and ice and, as has only recently been realised, offers great potential for winter climbing.

A German missionary was probably the first white man to catch a distant view of Kenya, but his tales of snow-capped mountains in Eastern Africa were greeted with scepticism and it was not until 1883 that the Scottish naturalist, Joseph Thomson, exploring the Aberdare Mountains in Masai territory to the west caught sight, through a rugged depression, of 'a gleaming snow-white peak with sparkling facets which scintillated with the superb beauty of a colossal diamond'. The vision lasted a brief moment before, as he wrote, 'a moisture laden breeze touched the peak, wove a fleecy mantle and gradually enshrouded the heaven-like spectacle'.

Various explorers followed, then in 1899 a large expedition led by Sir Halford Mackinder and Campbell Hausburg set off with two Courmayeur guides and the definite intent of scaling the mysterious peak. Following an awkward route across the South Face of Nelion, Mackinder and his two Italians, Brocherol and Ollier, crossed a steep hanging ice-field and scrambled to the summit of Batian. Mackinder christened the ice-field 'Diamond Glacier', a particularly apt and beautiful name in view of the diamond-hard texture of the ice and the way it is set between the two peaks like a jewel.

Thirty years passed before the mountain was climbed again. Eric Shipton and Percy Wyn Harris both at the time working in Kenya made the second ascent in 1929, taking in the summit of Nelion as well. The following year with another British ex-patriot, Bill Tilman, Shipton climbed the long Northwest Ridge of Batian, today considered the greatest of the mountain's classic routes.

A famous attempt was made on the mountain in 1943 by three Italian prisoners of war, escaped from nearby Nanyuki. Eluding security and with stolen rations and improvised equipment, they made a spirited assault and reached Point Lenana, the lower third summit. In recent years many long and hard rock and mixed routes of alpine style have been added, mostly by British and Austrian climbers—among them the Diamond Couloir and the Ice Window which must rank among the most intriguing ice climbs in the world.

Half Dome (8852 ft/2698 m)
Yosemite Valley,
Sierra Nevada, California, USA (Plate 30)

Yosemite Valley with its sculpted crags and spires of perfect granite, its woods and waterfalls, is world-famous, tourists flock to gaze at its wonders and have done so in ever-increasing numbers for more than a century. Dominating the head of the valley is great Half Dome, an

Half Dome

impressively steep, round-topped mountain which, as its name suggests, appears to have been sliced abruptly in half. Geological surveyors in 1865 declared that Half Dome was perfectly inaccessible and was the one of all the Yosemite summits which would never be trodden by human foot. Such a rash statement was bound to arouse great interest in scaling the peak and the first attempts were made soon afterwards. In 1875 a remarkable Scot, George Anderson, a one-time sailor and carpenter, set himself to climb the curving Northeast Face, where a shoulder of rock leads easily to half height. From the shoulder he laboriously drilled a line of holes, placing in them bolts he had forged at his camp below. To these he fixed a hand-line and after weeks of work finally reached the top! Today a series of fixed cables at waist height following much the same route, enables tourists, with a strong head for heights, to mount Half Dome under their own steam.

In Europe during the nineteen-thirties many of the large rock walls of the Dolomites and Eastern Alps were climbed using the newly-developed aid techniques, and eventually Californian climbers began applying similar methods, using many pitons and expansion bolts, to their own beetling walls. The delicate needle of Lost Arrow was climbed thus in 1947 by John Salathé, an emigré Swiss blacksmith, and Anton Nelson. Salathé had evolved a new type of hard steel peg specially for the cracks in the Yosemite granite and which could be used again and again—it was vastly superior to the European soft steel pegs in general use. This and other technical developments revolutionised Yosemite climbing and by the mid-fifties the stage was set for a further advance, and climbers began to examine the sheer cut-away side of the Dome, the Northwest Face. Royal Robbins with Jerry Gallwas and Mike Sherrick forced a way to the top in five tense days in 1957, following a meandering line on the left side of the forbidding 2000 foot (600 m) face, the first Grade VI climb in North America. Later Robbins pioneered three more routes on the same face, notably Tis-sa-ack—taking eight days and using 110 bolts—in 1968. During the last decade there has been a move to clean up routes, and placing nuts has taken over from pegging with the first 'all-nut' ascent of the Northwest face taking place in 1973. In 1977 a very hard new route on the righthand side of the Face was established by Jim Bridwell and Dale Bard.

Mount McKinley (20,322 ft/6194 m)
Alaska, USA

Mount McKinley is the highest mountain in North America. Its Indian

Mount McKinley

name is 'Denali', the Great One, and from the wide, boggy tundra to the north, almost at sea level, the massif rises a full 17,000 feet (5000 m) in 12 miles (20 km). Glaciers flow from its slopes right down to the tree line. The complete McKinley range extends some 150 miles (240 km) from Rainy Pass to the Nenana River with less than twenty other summits over 10,000 feet (3000 m) and McKinley itself, vast yet shapely, completely dwarfing the lesser peaks. Five major ridges and a complex array of spurs and buttresses spring from its two summits, cradling numerous basins of snow, tortured icefalls and five huge glaciers. Proximity to the Arctic Circle guarantees extremely low temperatures, while proximity to the sea brings terrible storms—the muggy warm Pacific winds collide with the cold polar air masses right over McKinley. Long periods of clear, calm skies are rare.

The first attempt to climb the mountain was made in 1903 by Judge Wickersham of Fairbanks with a small party, but they did not get very far. Then in 1906 came Dr Frederick Cook with two companions. After losing their way in the confused wilderness south of the peak, Cook decided to go on alone with a hired porter. Several weeks later he returned claiming to have reached the top of McKinley and showing photographs reputedly taken on the summit, a claim later proved to be completely bogus. The first authentic ascent was by Hudson Stuck and his party in 1913, although an adventurous group of prospectors the 'Sourdoughs' had climbed the lower, North Summit, in 1910. Both of these parties climbed by the Muldrow Glacier and Karstens Ridge, and this was the route followed by all subsequent expeditions until 1951 when Bradford Washburn, who had made a careful study of the mountain, pioneered the West Buttress route above the Kahiltna Glacier. This proved a shorter and more popular climb. Today there are more than a dozen other lines on the mountain, four of them on the awesome South Face, originally known as 'Impossible Wall'. In 1961 the famous Italian mountaineer, Riccardo Cassin, led a powerful team up a ridge in the centre of this face, a mixed climb of over 10,000 feet (3000 m) which took two weeks and used siege tactics. Nowadays it is usually climbed alpine-style and has actually been soloed.

Two separate routes were traced on the Wickersham Wall, the northern flank in 1963; Hans Gmoser led a Canadian party up the right-hand side of the face and a month later a Harvard group put a route in the centre of the Wall. In 1967 McKinley's first winter ascent was made; one climber died in a crevasse on the Kahiltna Glacier on the approach, but the others pressed on and Art Davison, Dave Johnson and Ray Genet reached the summit after four weeks. On the return they were trapped on the Denali Pass by bad weather for six days, before struggling down to find their base camp deserted, their companions having pulled out, believing them dead.

Dougal Haston and Doug Scott climbed the South Face in May 1976, first following the '67 American Direct line, then continuing, in bad weather, by a new route parallel to the Cassin Ridge.

Cerro Torre (10,280 ft/3133 m)
Patagonia, Argentina

In the wastes of Patagonia, lashed by Antarctic storms and where, even in midsummer, the winds can accelerate to a hundred miles an hour within minutes, a cluster of bizarre granite towers rises—none stranger than the dramatic finger of Cerro Torre. Reinhold Messner has described it as a Scream Turned into Stone. One of the Fitzroy Group to the East of the Patagonian Ice Cap it is generally considered to be one of the most difficult mountains in the world, savage and remote. The Group's highest mountain, Fitzroy itself, was first climbed in 1952 by a French expedition and Azema's expedition book described the 'nightmare aiguille of Cerro Torre, emerging from a bubbling devil's cauldron of cloud, like a glittering lighthouse.' Other climbers soon came to see for themselves. Two Italian expeditions in 1958 tried Cerro Torre without success, then in 1959 a spectacular first ascent was claimed. Césare Maestri, an Italian, and Toni Egger from Austria, after establishing three camps over the glaciers leading to the foot of the 5000 foot (1500 m) East Face, climbed to the Col of Conquest and embarked on an alpine-style assault on the North Face. Six days after they had set off, a companion, still awaiting their return, found Maestri half-buried in snow, alone and confused on the glacier. They had reached the summit, Maestri claimed, but during the descent Egger had been swept away by an avalanche. Years later, as more and more climbers attempted Cerro Torre and failed, people began to question whether Maestri and Egger could really have been to the summit at all. As if to defy the sceptics, Maestri returned to Cerro Torre in 1970, this time climbing the Southeast Ridge and East Face of the mountain climbing a line of bolts which he placed with a compressed-air drill! Outraged, climbers around the world condemned such tactics on so fine a mountain. By his own admission, Maestri had not this time attempted the overhanging ice mushroom on the summit, and so this could not be considered a true ascent. Finally, in the winter of 1973–4 another Italian team, led by

Cerro Torre

Casimiro Ferrari, climbed the West Face *and* the final crown of ice, and stood, indisputably atop Cerro Torre. But were they the first? Their ascent did not answer the question — had Maestri and Egger stood there 15 years before? Maestri still sticks to his story which has remained unchanged over the years even after numerous probing interviews. In 1975 Toni Egger's body was discovered a mile and a half down the glacier from where it had fallen, but his camera, which may have contained vital summit evidence, was never found. Unless and until it is, the enigma can never be positively solved. In 1978 Maestri's 'bolt-ladder' was repeated alpine-style in a remarkable $1\frac{1}{2}$ days by Americans Jim Bridwell and Steve Brewer.

Alpamayo (19,510 ft/5947 m)
Cordillera Blanca,
Peru

Though it is not the highest, Alpamayo is probably the best-known mountain in Peru. It is breathtakingly lovely and has, with reason, often been dubbed the most beautiful mountain in the world. Seen from the northwest, it rises as a perfect pyramid, but from the south-west it is exquisite — a slender trapezoid, draped in fluted ice. These strange chiselled flutings are caused by moist masses of air rising from the Amazon basin coupled with the effect of the tropical sun beating vertically down on the ice. It gives the mountain the aspect of a gleaming gothic cathedral.

The Cordillera Blanca was mapped by the celebrated Austrian cartographer, Erwin Schneider, in the thirties and he published photos of an 'unknown mountain in the Alpamayo Valley'. A Swiss expedition came to attempt the heavily-corniced North Ridge in 1948, but close to the top, a cornice broke and they plunged down the 650 foot (200 m) face. Miraculously they were unharmed, but they did not return to the attack! In 1951 a strong Franco-Belgian expedition again tried the North Ridge, cautiously detouring onto the East Face wherever possible to avoid the massive cornices. They reached the top as darkness fell and only later learned that they had reached the North summit — the higher true summit still lay some 600 delicate feet (180 m) ahead along the almost horizontal crest. Learning of this error, a German team took up the challenge in 1957, they chose the unknown South Ridge and despite miserable weather, eventually made the first true ascent of Alpamayo.

Alpamayo

46

A British expedition in 1966, led by Dennis Gray, climbed the North Ridge and successfully traversed the airy connecting ridge to the Main Summit. In the years that followed, other routes were tried, traverses were made by German and New Zealand parties and in 1975 the 3000 foot (900 m) Southwest Face itself was climbed by a strong Italian team led by Casimiro Ferrari (who had previously climbed Cerro Torre). Fixing ropes to within 650 feet (200 m) of the top and climbing only when the face was in shadow, six climbers reached the summit. Two years later the remarkable French climber, Nicholas Jaeger, soloed the same face—seven hours up and down! And in 1979 a new route was made on the Southeast Face by a Yugoslav team who found the angle of the ice to be 80° in places.

Nanda Devi (25,645 ft/7816 m)
Garhwal Himalaya, India

Nanda Devi—the Goddess Nanda, Goddess of Bliss—is one of the most beautiful and secretive of mountains. It is surrounded by a protective ring of rugged peaks, a 70 mile (110 km) barrier with no less than 19 summits over 21,000 feet (6400 m). Early explorers tried in vain to penetrate this 'Sanctuary'. There is only one breach in the wall, the Rishi Ganga Gorge to the west, a fearsome spot steeped in local legend, the home, it is said, of the Seven Rishis or Sages where, guarded by a serpent, they meditate unmolested. Nearby is supposed to be a great pile of shoes, all that remains of the unwary travellers the serpent has devoured!

W.W. Graham in 1883 and T.G. Longstaff some twenty years later tried unsuccessfully to force a passage through this gorge. Longstaff did manage to climb a col to the east and was rewarded by a view into the Sanctuary, but it was not until 1934 that Eric Shipton and Bill Tilman forced a route through the Rishi Gorge and finally entered the inner sanctum. They spent six weeks exploring and mapping and having reconnoitred the South Ridge of Nanda Devi to a height of 20,000 feet (6000 m), concluded that a well-equipped party would have a strong chance of success. But it was Everest that was occupying the minds of climbers of the day and a big expedition had been planned for 1936. Two climbers who were not selected for Everest were Tilman, who was thought unlikely to acclimatise well, and Noel Odell, who was considered too old at 45—despite having done well in 1924. Instead they

Nanda Devi

put together a small Anglo-American expedition to Nanda Devi, followed the route reconnoitred in 1934, and reached the top with little problem. The 'rejects' had seized as a prize the highest summit in the British Empire and which for 14 years remained the highest mountain ever climbed!

Forty years passed. Nanda Devi East peak had been climbed in 1939 by a Polish expedition, and two Frenchmen had disappeared in 1951 attemping a bold traverse of the long ridge linking Nanda Devi summit with Nanda Devi East but no new route had been successfully completed. A two-way attempt on the traverse by an Indo-French expedition in 1975 also failed, but the route was finally completed by Japanese climbers in 1976, the same year that Americans returned to the mountain. Co-leaders were Adams Carter, a veteran of the 1936 ascent, and Willi Unsoeld, whose first sight of the mountain in 1949 had so impressed him that he named his first daughter Nanda Devi. Now grown, she too was a member of this latest expedition. An important and difficult new route was attempted, the North Ridge, and Reichardt, Roskelley and States reached the summit. However, on a second bid, Nanda Devi Unsoeld died high on the mountain from an undiagnosed abdominal complaint.

Dhaulagiri I (26,795 ft/8167 m)
Dhaula Himal,
West Nepal

The Dhaulagiri massif lies to the west of the Kali Gandaki River in West Nepal. For the first half of this century Nepal was closed to outsiders and it was not until after 1949 that the remote areas of Western Nepal were explored for the first time. The topography of the Dhaula Himal is very complex and has often given rise to confusion. On one occasion, for instance, an expedition attempting—as they thought—an ascent of Dhaulagiri IV, later realised that they had in fact tried Dhaulagiri VI!

In 1950, Maurice Herzog's French expedition, explored various eastern approaches above the Kali Gandaki gorges and entered the Hidden Valley, north of Tukucha, but unable to get to grips with Dhaulagiri itself they recrossed the river to make the first ascent of Annapurna to the east. This was the first 'Eight-thousander' to be climbed and, one by one, the others followed—Everest, Nanga Parbat, K2, Cho Oyu, Kangchenjunga, and so on, until by the end of the nine-

Dhaulagiri I

teen-fifties only two of the fourteen remained virgin—Shisha Pangma and Dhaulagiri. The former was within forbidden Tibet, but Dhaulagiri had been tried by six expeditions and had repulsed them all. Finally, in 1960, the Swiss mountaineer, Max Eiselin, led an international expedition and, using a light aircraft (which later crashed) to assist in transporting stores to the North East Col, eventually forced the ridge above it to the summit. It was a fine achievement and eight men reached the top.

Other expeditions, particularly Japanese, continued exploring in the range and many of the lesser peaks were climbed: Tukucha, Gurja Himal, D VI, Churen Himal, Sita Chichura, Gama Peak, D II, Putha Hiunchuli, and D III, and it was not until 1969 that Dhaulagiri itself was again attemped, this time by an American expedition. But there was tragedy. Five Americans and two Sherpas perished in an ice avalanche and only one climber, Lou Reichardt, survived. Dhaulagiri's second ascent was finally made by Japanese climbers in 1970 and the Americans who reached the summit in 1973 were Reichardt, the survivor from 1969, with John Roskelley and Nawang Sherpa.

Meanwhile success was proving elusive on D IV. Five Austrians and a Sherpa died in a 1969 attempt, several Japanese expeditions tried, losing one climber, another Austrian expedition was unsuccessful, two men had been killed on a British attempt in 1973 while three Sherpas died in an avalanche during the RAF expedition in 1974. Finally, two Japanese reached the summit in the following spring, but both were lost on the descent. Finally another Japanese expedition that autumn placed ten men on the summit without mishap. D V was also climbed that same year.

Using a new approach route, Reinhold Messner brought a small expedition to the awesome South Face in 1977, the white wall overlooking the Nepalese jungle. Desperately steep, it rises 13,000 feet (4000 m) and is constantly swept by avalanches. Messner failed, but a route was put up on the face by Japanese climbers the following year. In 1979 yet another Japanese expedition, led by a woman, Dr. Michiko Takahashi, after establishing intermediate camps, completed a traverse over the summits of D II, D III and D V, the first-ever expedition to link three major Himalayan peaks.

K2—Chogori or Mount Godwin Austen
(28,253 ft/8611 m)
Baltoro Muztagh, Karakorum Range, Pakistan

The history of the Karakorum is closely connected with the 'Great Game' and the first Europeans on the Baltoro glacier were surveyors—like Godwin Austen in the 1860s—or operatives like Younghusband a few years later. Climbers first came in 1892 when Martin Conway's large expedition explored the Baltoro, Hispar and Biafo Glaciers and in 1909 when the Duke of Abruzzi's Italian expedition made a comprehensive reconnaissance of K2. The fine photographs bought back by Vittorio Sella from the expedition generated much interest in the Baltoro peaks.

But one attempt had already been made on K2 in 1902, when an international team led by Oscar Eckenstein and including Aleister Crowley, 'The Great Beast' of witchcraft fame, attempted the Northeast Ridge, reaching a height of about 21,400 feet (6500 m). Abruzzi's expedition climbed the Southeast—or 'Abruzzi'—Spur to a height of 22,000 feet (7000 m), and also reached the Savoia Saddle and Windy

K2 – Chogori or Mount Godwin Austen

Gap. All were ahead of their time. In 1938 an American Reconnaissance Expedition reached 26,000 feet (8000 m) on the Abruzzi Spur and the following year the Americans returned. Fritz Wiessner and his sherpa, Pasang Dawa Lama, made two summit bids, reaching a height of 27,500 feet (8380 m) from a Camp 9 before being beaten back—only to discover that, apart from a sick Dudley Wolfe who awaited them in Camp 8, the whole mountain had been evacuated, and all provisions and sleeping bags had been taken down! Wiessner and Pasang had an epic retreat—to base camp, leaving Wolfe marooned high on the mountain, before they found their team mates. Three Sherpas returned to rescue him, but neither they nor Wolfe were ever seen again.

In 1953 the Americans returned to K2, led again by Dr. Charles Houston who had also led the 1938 attempt. They reached 25,400 feet (7800 m)—Camp 8—before a blizzard forced a terrible and epic retreat during which one of their number, the geologist Art Gilkey, already stricken by thrombosis, was swept away in an avalanche. The following year a large expedition led by Professor Desio of Milan renewed the Italian interest in the mountain. No expense was spared and a very strong team of climbers gathered for the assault once again via the Abruzzi Spur. Their efforts were rewarded and on 31 July, A. Compagnoni and L. Lacedelli stood on the summit of the second highest mountain in the world.

American climbers failed in a bid to climb the Northwest Ridge in 1975, and Poles were narrowly beaten on the Northeast Ridge in 1976. A second ascent of the Abruzzi Spur was made the following year by Japanese climbers, and in 1978, Chris Bonington abandoned a British attempt on one of the west ridges after Nick Estcourt was lost in an avalanche. A few weeks later, however, a large American team made an ascent by a new route, following the Northeast Ridge to just below the summit pyramid, then traversing the East Face to complete the climb by the Abruzzi Spur. In 1979 a massive French expedition attempting the SSW Ridge were forced to give up when less than 500 feet (150 m) from the summit because of appalling weather; the Abruzzi Spur had been repeated a few weeks earlier in fast time by Reinhold Messner's small expedition.

Top left: Edward Whymper

Top Right: A. F. Mummery

Centre Left: Geoffrey Winthrop Young

Bottom Left: F. S. Smythe

Bottom Right: Fred Beckey

Top Left: Hermann Buhl

Top Right: Don Whillans

Centre Right: Tom Patey

Bottom Left: Dougal Haston

Bottom Right: Reinhold Messner

4
Men in High Places

Edward Whymper (1840-1911)

When Edward Whymper began his alpine career, the Victorian 'Golden Age' of mountaineering was almost over. Most of the major peaks in the Alps had been climbed, with the one obvious and tempting exception of the Matterhorn, which remained an elusive and glittering prize. Whymper was an artist-engraver and first came to the Alps at the age of 20 to make a series of illustrations for a book. Though he had no previous experience, he soon discovered a talent and enthusiasm for climbing mountains and returned to the Alps for several summers following, making quite a reputation for himself with his bold new ascents. But it was the Matterhorn that beguiled him, and he launched an obsessive siege upon its flanks, making no less than seven attempts from the Italian side, only to be repeatedly repulsed by bad weather or climbing difficulties. On one solo attempt, he tumbled 200 feet (60 m) and was badly injured. Finally, in 1865, he decided to try the Zermatt ridge and his fortune changed. The summit was gained at last but what should have been a glorious success was marred by tragic consequences. The climb had in fact developed into a race once it became known that a strong Italian team, led by Jean-Anthoine Carrel, had already set off from Breuil on the other side of the mountain. In Zermatt, too, was another British team about to launch an attempt and, not wishing to wait, Whymper suggested they join forces. Thus it was that on 13 July Whymper set off with a scratch party of seven men, united by providence and little else. That night they bivouacked at 11,000 feet (3300 m) in high spirits and began again at dawn. Climbing steadily they reached the summit at 1.40 p.m. and were delighted to find its snow untrodden; the Italian party were still away below. Seeking to attract their attention, they yelled until they were hoarse and in a frenzy of triumph, hurled rocks and boulders down onto their hapless competitors who turned and fled. Hardly a friendly gesture! But it is easy to understand their exuberance at last to have achieved this long-cherished ideal. Joy was short-lived, however. Less than an hour after leaving the summit, the youngest, and most inexperienced in the party, Douglas Hadow, slipped, dragging with him two other Britons and the Chamonix guide, Michel Croz. The rope broke, leaving Whymper and two Swiss clinging to the mountainside as the others plunged to their deaths. This accident triggered international condemnation and it had a profound effect on the young Whymper. In his own words 'there was never glad confident morning again'. He became dour and aloof, pedantic to the point of cantankerousness. He had never had a gift for making friends and thus remained solitary despite later successes. Though he never took part in serious high alpine climbing again, he visited the Andes and realised a boyhood dream by exploring in Greenland. He even climbed the Matterhorn once more, making the 72nd ascent in 1874 with, as his guide, Jean-Anthoine Carrel, the man from whom he had snatched success nine years before. Whymper was a master of painstaking documentation and wrote books of his travels and scientific observations.

A.F. Mummery (1855-1895)

Albert Mummery is often described as The Father of Modern Mountaineering. He brought a new approach to climbing, an audacity which indeed seems to belong more to this century than the last and his influence is still felt today. Writing a book on Victorian Mountaineers, Ronald Clark deliberately omitted Mummery because he considered him to be 'so much of the modern spirit as not to be a true Victorian'! And Reinhold Messner, re-reading Mummery's writings before his solo Nanga Parbat climb in 1978, remarked: 'What this man did more than 80 years ago is quite unbelievable. The more I read his letters, the more I am amazed by him. . . . he seems to have anticpated my thoughts by almost a century.'

Mummery was born in Kent in 1855; he was a frail child with a weakness of the spine that never left him, so he was unable to carry a heavy pack. He was also very short-sighted and friends recall that he preferred not to wear his pebble glasses on easy terrain with the result that he was 'much given to tumbling down on a path'. Add to this a tall and lanky frame and one does not get the picture of a leading mountaineer, described as a gymnast of almost unique skill. Yet, the fact remains that Mummery pioneered many fine new routes which are amongst the best-loved classic climbs of today. Initially he climbed with top guides, notably Alexander Burgener, but around 1890, preferring the company of a few friends, he began 'guideless climbing'. This was considered an almost heretical concept at the time but is nowadays taken for granted.

Mummery was first captivated by mountains on an alpine holiday at the age of 16 and the Matterhorn particularly inspired him. 'It seemed the very embodiment of mystery,' he wrote, and it remained one of his favourite peaks. He first climbed it three years later and in 1879 took part in the first ascent of its Zmutt Ridge. A year later he climbed it by another new route, the Furggen Ridge. However, he was forced to abandon the ridge and finish the climb by the East Face and it was another 61 years before anyone climbed the complete ridge. Mummery went to the Caucasus in the years 1888 and 1890, where, amongst other fine climbs, he made the first ascent of Dykh-Tau with Heinrich Zurfluh.

In 1895 he visited Nanga Parbat in the Himalaya with his friends Collie, Hastings, Bruce and two Gurkha soldiers. This was the first-ever attempt to climb one of the giant 8,000-metre peaks. Having ascertained that the sheer southern flank of the mountain, the Rupal Face, offered no hope of success, Mummery launched an attempt from the Diamirai Valley. He observed a series of rock ribs running up the centre of the face which seemed the only safe passage from the continual raking avalanches. Mummery and one of the Gurkhas, Raghobir Thapa, forced a route up the central spur of this great rib system and established a small tent with stores at 17,800 feet (5400 m) and a food dump at 20,000 feet (6000 m). On their final attempt, Raghobir was taken ill above this last dump just below the final ice barrier. Mummery, convinced that they stood at the gateway to success and bitterly disappointed, led his sick companion back off the mountain. Time was running short and it was decided, before returning home, to make one final attempt from the north. While the rest of the party took the equipment round the longer, lower route, Mummery and the two Gurkhas attempted a direct crossing by a high snow pass, the Diama Col. They were never seen again and it is supposed they perished under an avalanche.

(The 'Mummery Rib' was finally climbed to the summit by Reinhold Messner in 1978. Messner had previously descended with his brother by a similar route eight years before.)

Geoffrey Winthrop Young (1876-1958)
Throughout much of the 19th century most 'real' climbing was done in the Alps—'The Playground of Europe' and the British hills were not considered mountaineering areas in their own right but merely practice grounds for skills first learned abroad. But towards the turn of the century attitudes changed and British hills and crags were recognised as having an interest of their own. Routes began to appear on Welsh and Lakeland rock, mainly following the lines of marked gulleys. This was the climate then when Winthrop Young began climbing. By the time he first went to the Alps in 1897 he had been walking and rock-climbing for many years in the hills of Ireland, Wales and the Lake District, and he never lost his love of British mountains.

In the Alps, new routes were being ventured on the harder ridges and faces. Young claimed his share, becoming the leading British force in the

Alps during the years running up to World War 1. He climbed sometimes with friends and sometimes with guides. His most constant companion, with whom he pioneered many fine routes, was Josef Knubel of
St. Niklaus. Though technically this was a guide/client relationship, it
was at the same time the perfect partnership—Young had a knack for
spotting a route and realising the strategy required to tackle it, Knubel
was the supreme craftsman on rock and ice. Their routes included:
Taschhorn SW Face, the Younggrat on the Breithorn, the Zinal Rothorn
East Face, Grandes Jorasses West Ridge, Knubel Crack on the Mer de
Glace Face of the Grépon, and the Rote Zahn Ridge on the Gspaltenhorn.
With Mallory and Robertson, Young climbed the Northeast Ridge of
the Nesthorn and with H.O. Jones the great Brouillard Ridge on Mont
Blanc.

Then came World War 1 and alpine activity was interrupted. Young
served with ambulance units, winning awards for gallantry, and then in
the Battle of Monte San Gabriele was severely wounded and lost his
left leg above the knee. It seemed impossible that he would ever again
mountaineer, yet such was his tenacity and love of mountains, that he
learned, slowly and painfully, to climb once more. He wrote an account
of his one-legged climbs in his book *Mountains With a Difference*.

Winthrop Young was a gifted poet and writer, he was also a philoso-
pher and conversationalist and could draw a brilliant circle of friends
around him. His famous parties at the Pen y Pass inn in North Wales
brought together the most talented young climbers and the sharpest
intellects of his day. He had a feeling for tradition but also an eye to
the future and he foresaw the great explosion that would take place in
the sport of mountaineering as it became open to more than merely the
privileged classes. He saw a need for a single voice to speak for mountaineers in Britain and it was largely through his efforts that the British
Mountaineering Council came into being. He remainded a monumental
influence on the climbing scene long after making his own considerable
contribution to its history. His books, particularly *Mountain Craft* and
On High Hills, are still regarded as classics of mountain literature.

F.S. Smythe (1900-1949)
Frank Smythe's fame as a mountaineer spread beyond the climbing
fraternity to a much wider audience because he was an expert photo-
grapher and could write well about his mountain adventures. Rather
like Reinhold Messner today, he was often accused of 'courting publicity', no doubt by contemporaries envious of his success. In those
days it was not at all usual—as it is today—for climbers to make a liveli-
hood from their sport, but Smythe from the age of 27 was able to live

by lecturing and writing. In all he produced 15 books on mountaineering, including one novel, and published 10 volumes of photographs. He tried to explain not just what it was like to climb, but to give an idea of the atmosphere of the hills and an insight into the mind of the climber. Though some of his ideas might seem romantic to us today, many are the climbers who were first inspired by the writings of Smythe.

He was a weak child who was not allowed to play games at school because of a murmur in his chest. Shy and sensitive, he became a solitary boy. From the age of 15 he spent his summer holidays rambling alone over the hills of North Wales, then at 19, as a student in Bradford, he joined the Yorkshire Ramblers Club and went out regularly with other young climbers. Later he studied for two years in Austria and this gave him the opportunity for alpine winter and summer climbing and to learn ski-touring. In 1927, having been invalided out of the RAF, he spent a long season in the Mont Blanc range where he climbed the difficult East Ridge of the Aiguille du Plan with J.H.B. Bell (2nd ascent Ryan-Lochmatter route), which he later described as his hardest rock climb. Then with Professor T. Graham Brown he made the first ascent of the Red Sentinel route on Mont Blanc's formidable Brenva Face, and the following year, the Route Major, another splendid line on the same face.

In 1930 Smythe took part in Professor Dyhrenfurth's International Kangchenjunga Expedition and the next year organised his own expedition to Kamet in Garhwal. It was an outstanding success and Kamet became the world's highest summit yet reached. Consequently in 1933 when a team was being selected to attempt Everest, Frank Smythe and all members of his Kamet expedition were invited to join. Smythe proved to be one of the ablest of the team and it was generally believed that, had there not been a misunderstanding about establishing Camp 5, he and Shipton might well have got to the top that year before the weather broke. As it was, Smythe, climbing alone, equalled the height reached by Norton in 1924, about 28,125 feet (8570 m). He went again to Everest in 1936 and 1938, and in 1937 spent a successful season in the Garhwal Himalaya where he visited the 'Valley of Flowers', collecting some 250 Himalayan plant species. After World War 2 he explored in the Canadian Rockies and Lloyd George Range, and was planning to spend six months in the Himalaya in 1949 when he was taken ill in India and died soon afterwards.

Fred Beckey (Born 1923)
Fred Beckey was born in Dusseldorf and moved to Seattle, USA, at the age of three. Summer camps with the Boy Scouts in the Olympic Moun-

1 The Sacred Mountain. Beautiful Machapuchare – the 'Fish's Tail' – is held in
veneration by the local people, and the Nepalese Government no longer allows
attempts to climb it. Its 22,958 ft/6998 m summit is still inviolate.

2 Mountains and Superstition. The ghostly Brocken Spectre was an object of dread in olden times. Here the Spectre is seen floating in the Gate of the Mists between the twin summit of Mount Kenya. (See also plate 33.)

3 Mountains and Religion. The Tibetan Buddhist monastery of Thyangboche is situated at an altitude of 12,700 ft/3870 m, beneath Ama Dablam (22,494 ft/6856 m) in Nepal's Khumbu Himalaya. (See also plate 37.)

4 Mountains and Mystery. The monks at Pangboche Gompa – or temple – near
Thyangboche where this treasure is carefully preserved, claim that it is the scalp
of a Yeti or 'Abominable Snowman'.

5 Mountain Transport. The *Luftseilbahn* or *Téléferique* is ubiquitous nowadays throughout the European Alps. The cable-way here is on the Valluga (9216 ft/ 2809 m) above St Anton in the Lechtal Alps of N.W. Austria.

6   Today the helicopter is in general use as a maid-of-all-work in mountain regions. Here a member of Clint Eastwood's *The Eiger Sanction* film crew flies to work high on the Eiger itself.

7   There are many rack-railways still in operation in the world's mountain regions. This is the Snowdon Railway, built in 1896, which runs to the summit of the highest peak in England and Wales (3561 ft/1085 m).

8   Ski are the wherewithal of ski-mountaineering and ski-touring. Running down the Gefrornewand Glacier in Austria's Zillertal Alps, a climber returns from a spring ascent of the Olperer (11,401 ft/3475 m).

9   River crossing is often difficult in mountain terrain and spectacular suspension bridges are common throughout the Himalaya. This one spans the Balephi Khola in Nepal's Jugal Himal.

10 Man himself is the most reliable load carrier in many major mountain regions. This is especially true in the Himalaya where Nepalese porters are seen passing a wayside *chorten* – a sort of shrine.

11 Sometimes, however, specialised animals are used as beasts of burden; the llama for instance in the Andes, or the yak – as here – in Asia. The use of such animals is limited by steep ground and the availability of fodder.

12   Mountain People. The Bakonjo tribe from the Uganda slopes of the Ruwenzori –
the 'Mountains of the Moon' (see also plates 34, 58 & 59) – are hunters in the thick
montane forests. This lad's hat is of fur from the little mountain hyrax.

13   Many Tamangs, members of one of Nepal's hill tribes, are professional porters.
Here Tamang porters rest beside the trail up the Trisuli valley. In the distance is
Langtang Lirung (23,769 ft/7245 m). (See also plates 62 & 67.)

14 Joss Naylor, seen here with his dogs above his farm on the shores of Wastwater, is a shepherd and runs more than a thousand sheep on the fells of the English Lake District. (See also plate 39.)

15 The Sherpas of Nepal owe their affluence to their long specialisation as high-altitude porters. Kancha Sherpa, an expedition sardar or headman, is seen here with his family outside his house in Namche Bazar, the sherpa 'capital'.

16 The Mountains of England. The Lake District is a gentle landscape. The hamlet of Elterwater nestles at the entrance to the valley of Great Langdale; beyond are the Langdale Pikes with Harrison Stickle rising to 2403 ft/732 m.

17 The lush valley of Wasdale Head lies at the foot of Scafell – seen on the far right. To its left is Scafell Pike, at 3210 ft/978 m England's highest summit, and left again the Styhead Pass and Great Gable (2949 ft/899 m).

18 The Welsh Mountains. Snowdonia is wilder and more rugged than the Lake District and its mountains slightly higher. Tryfan (3010 ft/917 m) above the Ogwen Valley is reputedly the only summit outside Scotland that cannot be reached without the use of hands!

19 The sharp peak of Lliwedd (2947 ft/898 m) forms one arm of the famous Snowdon Horseshoe which cradles the lakes of Llydaw and Glaslyn. The Horseshoe is a noted ridge-walk. (See also plate 47.)

20 Many of Scotland's mountains stand close to the sea. These are the Black Cuillin on the Island of Skye, largest of the Hebrides, and they rise sheer over 3000 ft/ 900 m from the waters of Loch Scavaig.

21 Winter snows add a new dimension. The long and narrow summit crest of Liathach (3456 ft/1053 m) above Glen Torridon gives an expedition of almost alpine quality to the experienced scrambler.

22 It is June and the alpenglow lingers on the north-east crags of Ben Nevis (4406 ft/1343 m). There is good summer rock-climbing and world famous winter climbing on this, the highest of British mountains.

23   Mountains of the Alps. Typical of the larger snow and ice peaks is the Jungfrau –
the 'Maiden' – (13,642 ft/4168 m) in the Bernese Oberland of Switzerland, first
ascended in 1813. It is seen here from the north.

24 The Bregaglia group, on the Italian frontier in S.E. Switzerland, showing the Piz Badile (10,853 ft/3308 m) with its classic North Ridge dropping towards camera and its famous N.E. Face on the left. (See also plate 54.)

25 Mountains of Canada. Except in the far north, North American mountains tend to be 'alpine' in character and size. The north ridge of Mount Assiniboine (11,870 ft/ 3618 m) – the 'Matterhorn of the Rockies' – towering over the British Columbia/ Alberta border, was first climbed in 1903. (See also plates 55 & 57.)

26 In the Interior Ranges of British Columbia rise the granite peaks of the Bugaboos. This is Bugaboo Spire (10,450 ft/3185 m) with its classic S. Ridge as the right-hand skyline. Leftward are the Bobby Burns mountains.

27 Mount Robson, at 12,972 ft/3954 m, is the highest summit in the Rockies and was first climbed in 1913. Today's regular route takes the S.S.W. Ridge, seen here falling diagonally right from the summit.

28 Mountains of America. Mount Whitney in California's beautiful Sierra Nevada –
    here seen from the north – is the highest peak in the contiguous United States
    (14,494 ft/4418 m). Its steep E. Face holds fine climbing on excellent granite.

29 Volcanoes, mostly dormant, dominate the Cascade Range of the Pacific North-
    west. This is Mount Hood (11,245 ft/3427 m) with, far left, the recently active
    Mount St Helens. Mounts Rainier and Adams are seen on the horizon.

30 Yosemite Valley, in the California Sierra, and its unique granite climbs are world famous. Half Dome's (8842 ft/2695 m) shadowed N.W. Face gives several notable 'big wall' climbs some 2000 ft/600 m in length.

31 In the deserts of the south western States rise many spectacular sandstone mountains and monoliths which often give incredible rock-climbs. This fine pinnacled butte stands above the Colorado River near Moab in Utah.

32 Mountains of Africa. The highest is Kilimanjaro, a dormant volcano, and its highest point is Kibo (19,340 ft/5895 m). The steep cliffs of rock and ice on Kibo's south western flank – on the left of the picture – give difficult climbs. (See plate 61.)

33 Ten miles south of the Equator, Mount Kenya rises in isolation to a series of rocky spires hung with tiny glaciers. Here the highest summit, Batian (17,085 ft/5199 m) is seen over Hut Tarn, with Point John (16,020 ft/4883 m) to the right. (See also plate 53.)

34 The Ruwenzori of Uganda and Zaire are the highest mountains to feed the Nile. These are the Coronation Peaks (Savoia – 16,330 ft/4977 m) of Mount Stanley seen from the north east. (See also plates 58 & 59.)

35 The Ultimate Mountains – the Himalaya. The crystal wall of the Annapurna Himal
    rises 23,000 ft/7000 m above the lakes and meadows of Pokhara in Nepal. These are
    the southern flanks of Annapurna II (26,041 ft/7937 m), right, and Annapurna IV
    (24,688 ft/7525 m).

36 A less known giant is Himalchuli (25,896 ft/7893 m) in Nepal's Gurkha Himal.
    Although ascended from the west by a Japanese team in 1960, the eastern flank
    seen here above the glen of the Chuling Khola, has not yet been climbed.

37 There are countless smaller peaks in the Himalaya – the graceful pyramid here is
    Ama Dablam (22,494 ft/6856 m) in the Khumbu Himal close to the foot of Mount
    Everest. (See also plate 3.) The lake is the Tshola Tsho.

38 Mount Everest, the highest mountain in the world (29,028 ft/8848 m) rises on the
    frontier of Nepal and Tibet and has now been climbed many times by four different
    routes and from both countries. The viewpoint is Gokyo Ri.

39 Fell Running is a competitive mountain sport popular in Britain. Here a noted fell-runner Joss Naylor (see plate 14) is seen bounding along the crest of Crib Goch in Snowdonia to break the Welsh '14 Peaks' record.

40 Hill Walking is a mountain sport for all the family. It can be gentle or energetic, but mountains should always be treated with due respect. The hills round Crafnant valley in Snowdonia are a good introduction to sterner stuff.

41 Trekking among the 'Greater Ranges' is a logical development of domestic Hill Walking. In the Himalaya of Nepal members of a trekking party ford the river below Gokyo Ri. (See plate 38.) Cho Oyu (26,750 ft/8153 m) rises beyond.

42   Sea-Cliff Climbing is especially popular in Britain where many miles of rocky coast give excellent sport. This is the chimney of the Direct Finish to 'Oche Slab' at Bosigran, in Cornwall, the spiritual home of the game.

43 Orkney's Old Man of Hoy is Britain's finest sea-stack, rising sheer 450 ft/137 m from the waves. Rusty Baillie, who made the first ascent in 1966, is seen on jumars on the E. Face – the regular route.

44 A popular sea-cliff is Craig Gogarth near Holyhead on Angelsey. Al Harris is climbing 'Dream of White Horses', a spectacular but not too desperate traverse round the walls of Wen Zawn.

45 Outcrop climbing is an enjoyable end in itself besides being good training for greater climbs. Ian Howell is seen in a desperate situation on Froggatt Edge, one of the many gritstone crags in the Derbyshire Peak District.

46 Rock-climbing in the English Lake District is second to none: with some justification it has been claimed that the sport was invented here. Ian Howell is leading 'Eliminate A' on Dow Crag above Lake Coniston.

47 This is 'Avalanche Route' on Lliwedd, an impressive 900 ft/270 m crag which is a satellite of Snowdon in North Wales. (See plate 19.) This route was pioneered by Archer Thomson in 1907.

48 Outcrop climbing in America. As in Britain climbs have been made almost any-where that there is rock. Rusty Baillie is climbing in the Granite Dells near Prescott in Arizona – small cliffs but great sport!

49 Ice-climbing is an art in itself and, in winter, the Scottish mountains can provide
    some of the world's best ice routes. The Direct Start to 'Aladdin's Mirror' in the
    Cairngorm's Coire an t'Sneachda, ascends this overhanging curtain of ice.

50 Creag Meaghaidh in the Central Highlands, although of little summer interest,
    is one of Scotland's best winter cliffs. Alan Fyffe and Jim MacArtney are at work
    on 'South Post Direct', a 1200ft/370 m route.

51 Bill March is making the first ascent of 'Window Gully' on the Lurchers Crag in the Cairngorms. From the narrow chimney behind the icicle he has cut his way out through the window to easier ground above.

52 Alpine Climbing may involve difficult technical work on rock, ice or mixed ground. The N. Face of the Doldenhorn, above Kandersteg in the Bernese Oberland, is an alpine ice route some 2300ft/700 m in length with only a narrow rock band to surmount near the top. Bill O'Connor is climbing.

53 The best alpine climbing in Africa is on Mt Kenya. (See plate 33.) This is the regular route to the two highest summits, Nelion and Batian. Nick Wood is approaching the bottom of Mackinder's Chimney.

54 One of the most famous rock routes in the Alps is Cassin's route on the N.E.
Face of the Piz Badile. (See plate 24.) First climbed over three days in 1937, this
3000 ft/1000 m climb is very sustained.

55. Alpine climbing in North America has an expeditionary flavour to it. High on the
N. Ridge, Bill March approaches the summit of Mount Assiniboine. On straightforward ground experienced climbers prefer to move quickly without the encum-
berance of the rope. (See plate 25.)

56 This is a long 'alpine' rock route at high altitude in the California Sierra. Gary
Colliver is seen at nearly 14,000 ft/4250 m on the 'Fish Hook Arete' of Mt Russell.

57 Mount Assiniboine's N. Ridge is not difficult, but a short and exposed rock step close below the summit requires extra care. (Plates 25 and 55). A hike of some 20 miles over a high pass is necessary to reach the mountain.

58 Climbing in the Ruwenzori is certainly expeditionary: though the peaks are 'alpine' and there are huts, the approach march takes three days! This is the summit of Kitasamba (15,950 ft/4862 m) above the Coronation Glacier. (Plate 34.)

59 Ruwenzori is noted for its weird ice formations. Jim Slade is rapelling to join John Temple in an ice cave below the Elena/Great Tooth Col of Mount Stanley.

60   Aid climbing is occasionally necessary on ice – for instance when negotiating glacier ice-falls. Bill March is seen at work on the Bugaboo Glacier in Canada. (Plate 26.)

61   The Kersten Glacier Direct is probably the finest pure ice route on Kilimanjaro. The approach march requires three bivouacs and the difficult climb itself another. After a bitter bivouac in this ice cave at some 17,500 ft/5350 m the welcome dawn creeps over the plains below.

62 In the Himalaya the scope for mountaineering of all kinds is still vast although most of the higher summits have now been reached. Right of centre is Langtang Lirung (23,769 ft/7245 m, see plates 13 and 67). Left is Shisha Pangma or Gosainthan (26,398 ft/8046 m). Both have been climbed.

63 Expeditionary mountaineering may necessitate the location and crossing of high
passes as well as the ascent of summits. This is the crossing of difficult 'Tilman's
Pass' (c. 17,400 ft/5300 m) in Nepal's Jugal Himal.

64   This picture was taken from the summit of 'Cathedral' on its first ascent. A fine granite obelisk a mere 17,000 ft/5200 m or so high, it gave a superb climb.

65 'Freney Peak' is some 19,000 ft/5600 m high and is a beautiful small ice peak in the Jugal Himal. This ice wall was the crux of the climb. Fast movement on rock, snow or ice is essential if such peaks are to be climbed 'alpine style'.

66 This is a 22,000 ft/6700 m summit in the Himalaya. While no longer 'alpine', climbing at this altitude is still enjoyable rather than masochistic. Fitness and good equipment are, of course, essential.

67 Two climbers approach the summit of a virgin and un-named rock needle in the Ganesh Himal after a straightforward but satisfying climb. Beyond is ubiquitous Langtang Lirung which dominates this part of Nepal. (Plates 13 & 62.)

68 High Altitude Mountaineering, especially on the largest peaks, requires good organization and months of preparation besides great feats of physical effort. This is Camp I on Mt Everest (c. 20,000 ft/6100 m) above the dangerous Khumbu Ice Fall.

69 The problems of High Altitude Climbing tend to be those of survival, route-finding and logistics rather than technical difficulty. Climbers approach the foot of the Great Couloir on Everest's S.W. Face. The tents of Camp III (c. 23,000 ft/7000 m) can be seen below the rock band to the right.

70 Loaded sherpas slog up Everest's Western Cwm at about 20,500 ft/6250 m. Ahead rises Lhotse (plate 38) and the South Col, with the huge face of Everest to the left – split by the Great Couloir up which lies the S.W. Face route.

71   The summit. One of the biggest thrills of mountaineering is to reach a summit
where no man has been before, but this is a prize given to few. The many delights
of mountaineering are hard to define but impossible to forget.

tains and the Cascades awakened an interest in mountaineering and by the age of sixteen he was making first ascents. At seventeen, with his younger brother Helmy, he penetrated the wilderness area of the Luna Cirque in the Northern Pickets where only two people had been before, and a couple of years later the boys, on a six-week expedition, make the second ascent of Mt Waddington in the British Columbia Coast Range, the 'Mystery Mountain' first discovered in the late twenties and climbed by Fritz Wiessner and Bill House in 1936.

During World War 2 Beckey was an instructor, training mountain troops, and his torrent of new climbs was interrupted, but in 1946 he was back, full of vigour, and made the first ascent of Devil's Tower in Wyoming. By this time his brother Helmy had 'retired' from climbing and there followed a long series of partners as the durable Beckey pioneered on with restless energy. His particular speciality has always been the wilderness of the Pacific Northwest—the Cascades, the Coast Range of British Columbia and Alaska—but there are few areas in North America where he has not established new routes. In a career spanning forty years he has made more than 300 first ascents and many consider him America's greatest mountaineer. He must surely be the most prolific. His climbs include: Kate's Needle, Mt Deborah, Mt McKinley Northwest Ridge, Mt Seattle, Snowpatch Spire East Face, Howser Spires West Face, first winter ascents of Mt Robson and Mt Sir Donald, Shiprock Southwest Spur in New Mexico, and the North Face of Mt Edith Cavell. In 1955 he made his sole journey to the Himalaya with an international expedition led by Norman Dyhrenfurth. The autumn conditions defeated them on their main objective, Lhotse, but Beckey was able to ski at 23,000 feet (6500 m) on the Khumbu Glacier and climbed other lesser peaks, including Langcha. He is the author of the *Climber's Guide to the Cascades and Olympics of Washington*.

Hermann Buhl (1924-1957)
Hermann Buhl was one of the best-known European climbers in the immediate post-war period. He came from Innsbruck in the heart of the mountains which he had first learned to love when walking with his father. Later he began rock climbing on the limestone crags of the Karwendel, the Kaiser and the Kalkkogel—all within easy reach. Physically he was not strong but he had remarkable powers of endurance and resolution. By the time he was 17 he was climbing the hardest Grade VI routes. He had a bad fall in 1943 when he strayed off-route on the Fleischbank and spent several weeks in hospital but recovered to make the first ascent of the Mauk West Face later that year. The war over, he began climbing in the Dolomites and then in the Western Alps to be-

come as much a master on snow and ice as he was on rock. He built up his stamina by undertaking phenomenally long alpine traverses, always driving himself very hard and often climbing solo. He was determined to discover just how far he could go. When he made his solo ascent of the Northeast Face of Piz Badile, he first cycled a hundred miles to reach the mountain, and returned the same way afterwards.

In 1953 Buhl was selected to go to Nanga Parbat with an expedition organised by Dr Karl Herrligkoffer. After four camps had laboriously been established on the mountain, a retreat was ordered but the weather was improving and Buhl with three others decided to defy the instruction and continue climbing. They set up Camp 5 at 22,600 feet (7200 m) and on 3 July Buhl set off towards the summit, still 4 miles ($6\frac{1}{2}$ km) away. His companion, leaving late, was unable to catch up and returned to camp. Buhl trudged on alone and, just at sunset, finally reached the summit. There was no way to retreat in the darkness and with no bivouac equipment, he was obliged to spend the night leaning against a rock. At dawn he pressed on, but it was not until 5.30 in the evening that he staggered into the arms of his companions above Camp 5. His ordeal had lasted 40 hours, and so emaciated was he that, in photographs taken on his return, he seemed to have aged 20 years, while his feet were so badly frostbitten that he eventually lost some of his toes. The climbing world was electrified when news of this dramatic first ascent became known and it is a lasting pity that Buhl's achievement was to be marred by acrimonious wranglings within the team and a court action by the expedition's leader.

In 1957 Buhl was a member of a four-man Austrian expedition which successfully made the first ascent of another 'Eight-thousander', Broad Peak in the Karakorum. Unlike other high-altitude climbs before, this was a lightweight, alpine-style ascent, pointing the way for the future. A few days later Buhl with Kurt Diemberger was caught in a bad storm high on nearby Chogolisa (25,110 ft/7650 m). Buhl, who had been leading, was behind Diemberger as they turned, unroped, to begin the descent. Diemberger, glancing round shortly afterwards, was horrified to see nothing but a set of footprints leading to the brink of the narrow cornice. Buhl had unbelievably walked off the mountain in the mist.

Don Whillans (Born 1933)

Don Whillans is one of the finest mountaineers to have emerged in postwar Britain. A tough Salford lad, in 1951 he met and teamed up with another Manchester climber, Joe Brown, and together they formed one of the most formidable partnerships ever seen in Britain. When 'The Rock and Ice' club was formed in Manchester in the summer of 1951 they were at its hub, and their activities on gritstone and in the Llanberis Pass and 'Cloggy' (Clogwyn Du'r Arddu) in Wales, soon passed into legend. They became known as the 'hard men' and under their influence British rock climbing took on a new impetus. As with Tom Patey, so many stories are related about Whillans that it is difficult to tell where fact stops and the myth starts—from Fort William to Kathmandu everyone has his personal favourite Whillans' tale and his flat 'at has passed into folklore. Tenacious, truculent, strong, caustic, humourous, straight, morose, mellow—Whillans is all these. He is the archetypal 'little man' who challenges the world head-on—and holds his ground. His Welsh routes with Brown include Cemetery Gates, Vember, Black Cleft, Taurus, and in Scotland, Sassenach on Ben Nevis where, with Bob Downes, he also put up Centurion. In the Alps Whillans and Brown made the first ascent of the West Face of Blaitière, and with Bonington, Clough and Dlugosz the first ascent of The Central Pillar of Frêney. Whillans took part in expeditions to Masherbrum and Trivor in the Karakorum, to Patagonia where he climbed Aiguille Poincenot and the Central Tower of Paine, to Guarisankar in Nepal and to Huandoy in Peru. In 1970, with Dougal Haston, Whillans reached the summit of Annapurna via the extremely formidable South Face: it was the first time a Himalayan giant had been climbed by a face route and it opened a new phase in Himalayan mountaineering. (The Rupal Face of Nanga Parbat was climbed a few weeks later by the Messner brothers and other members of the 'Siegi Löw Memorial Expedition'.) Whillans went twice to the Southwest Face of Everest but was not with the team that finally climbed it in 1974. Other expeditions have included Roraima in Guyana and Tirich Mir.

Tom Patey (1932-1970)

When Tom Patey was killed in a rappel accident on a Sutherland sea stack in 1970, the British climbing world reeled from the shock. It was not just that Patey was *the* Grand Master of Scottish mountaineering with a phenomenal record of exciting new summer and winter climbs, it was that he had a mammoth personality and sense of humour to match. The climbing world, like any other, desperately needs its rich characters and can ill afford to lose one as energetic and individual as Patey. His wryly observant writing and his ribald songs, irreverently lampooning his contemporaries, delighted fellow climbers.

Patey was particularly an explorer. He preferred new routes to old and had a flair for locating fresh cliffs and spotting the best lines on them. This was a talent he had developed in the fifties when, with a growing band of fellow Aberdonian climbers, he probed the potential of the Cairngorms, much-neglected as a climbing area before then. The rock was, as Patey preferred, not impeccably sound—it required guile and judgement to negotiate, and the gulleys and high corries offered great scope for fine winter routes. Patey's enthusiasm helped to inspire a vigorous new era in Scottish winter climbing. In a few years he had made more than 70 new routes in the Cairngorms alone and plenty more elsewhere in Scotland—including, with MacInnes and Nicol in five hours, the first ascent of Zero Gully on Ben Nevis, one of the truly great Scottish ice climbs and now of international repute. With his background of Scottish snow and ice Tom Patey was a superb mountaineer, and in the Alps he took part in many first British ascents, including the Sans Nom Arete of the Aiguille Verte and the North Face of the Aiguille du Plan. Later, climbing with various companions, he made a series of fine first ascents of mixed lines among the Chamonix Aiguilles and elsewhere in the Mont Blanc massif. In 1956 and 1958 Patey was in the Karakorum, first as a member of the successful small team which climbed the spectacular Mustagh Tower, and then with Mike Banks' expedition on Rakaposhi—where he again reached the summit. At that time he was a Surgeon-Lieutenant in the Marine Commandos, but he left the Navy in 1961 to enter general practice in Ullapool in Scotland's far Northwest.

Again he embarked on a fresh wave of exploration all over Britain from Cornwall to Cape Wrath. He had always preferred to climb with others, maintaining that good climbing and good company went together, but for want of companions in his remote home area he now often went solo and grew to enjoy it. Unroped, with MacInnes and others, he made the first winter traverse of the Cuillin Ridge in 1965, and he popularised the climbing of sea stacks, playing a leading role in the spectacular television documentary from the Old Man of Hoy. It was during the descent from one such stack, the Maiden, that he fell to his death.

In twenty years he had moved the centre of gravity of British climbing several hundred miles northwards.

Dougal Haston (1940-1977)

Dougal Haston was another product of the surge of climbing activity in Scotland in the fifties. He had begun climbing in his teens and soon teamed up with 'Big Eley' Moriarty. Living near Edinburgh they would practice on the now-famous Currie Railway Walls. They soon joined forces with a group of Edinburgh climbers, including Jimmy Marshall and Robin Smith, and were involved in many first ascents. By 1959 Haston had developed into a mature climber with a wealth of experience and a canny awareness in the hills. It was during that year that he took part in the first ascent of Ben Nevis' Minus Two Gully, then, returning from a fine first season in the Dolomites, climbed The Bat, a fierce rock route on the Ben, with Smith in September. When Smith was killed in the Pamirs in 1962, Haston took over his place as Scotland's leading young alpinist, and the next year made the second British ascent of the Eigerwand with Rusty Baillie. Early in 1966 he was a leading figure in the winter siege ascent of the Eiger Direct, a drama enacted in the full glare of publicity. After John Harlin, the American instigator of the climb, fell to his death, Haston and four Germans reached the summit during a raging blizzard. Afterwards, he took over Harlin's newly-formed International School of Mountaineering in Leysin, Switzerland, and from then on withdrew from the Scottish scene. Instead he extended his experience world-wide—joining an expedition to Cerro Torre, Patagonia, in 1969, making the first ascent of Annapurna South Face in 1970. In 1971, 1972 and 1975 he was on the Southwest Face of Everest, eventually being rewarded with the first ascent with Doug Scott. He also took part in the first ascent of Changabang in Garhwal in 1974, and in 1976 a new route on the South Face of Alaska's Mt McKinley, again with Scott. Haston had a reputation for wildness in his youth, but as he grew older he became thoughtful and introspective. Though shy, he learned to cope with publicity, lectured well, and had published two books and completed the first draft of a novel. At 37, the future seemed full of promise when one January afternoon he was killed in a powder snow avalanche whilst skiing alone above Leysin.

Reinhold Messner (Born 1944)
Reinhold Messner is frequently called the greatest active climber in the world today. Certainly no other person has ever reached the summits of so many of the world's mountain giants. He has six times been to the top of an 'Eight-thousander' and has climbed the highest point of every continent. All his ascents have been executed with style, one would almost say—panache.

One of nine children, native of the Italian South Tyrol, Messner was taken into the mountains by his parents from an early age. He vividly recalls his first easy climb at the age of five, it lit a passion that has never waned. Climbing regularly in his native Dolomites, he had, by the time he was 20, completed most of the popular hard routes. In 1969, when he was 25, he embarked on an incredibly creative alpine season, soloing climbs of the very highest calibre, often incorporating new route variations, and all in incredibly fast times. He was hailed as a sudden meteor in the climbing firmament, but in fact was displaying the results of a very long and thorough apprenticeship. His writing too was as bold and as prolific as his climbing. In outspoken articles he raged against the over-use of technical gadgetry which threatened to reduce mountaineering into a sort of engineering: it was 'Murder of the Impossible', he said.

Also in 1969 he went on his first overseas expedition—to the Peruvian Andes. With his friend Peter Habeler from Austria, he made the second ascent of the Northeast Face of Yerupaja in alpine style and also put up a new route on nearby Yerupaja Chico. The next year he and his younger brother Günther joined a large party to Nanga Parbat, organised by the veteran expedition-manager Dr Karl Herrligkoffer. After a long build-up of camps on the apallingly steep Rupal Face, the two brothers were the first to reach the summit. They bivouacked just below the top and in the morning, with Günther suffering badly from altitude sickness, decided they had no option but to retreat down the easier, but unprepared, Diamir Face of the mountain. It was a nightmare descent with Reinhold scouting ahead, then retracing his steps to lead his ailing brother down, and then, at the very base of the mountain, waiting in vain for Günther to catch up. Finally Reinhold realised that something serious had occurred and after hours of fruitless search, he was forced to accept that Günther must have been wiped out by an avalanche. It was this sad event and his lonely struggle back to civilisation, followed by spiteful wrangles with other members of the team, that helped shape the pattern of his later life. Since then, Messner has vehemently rejected dependence on other people and obsessionally limited his climbing equipment. He has been ready to test his theories pratically, ranging all over the world in pursuance of his ideals. Having climbed Manaslu in 1972, he and Habeler became the first two-man party ever to climb an Eight-thousander with their lightweight raid on Hidden Peak. Though he had never used oxygen equipment on any of his climbs, Messner was glad of the opportunity to attempt Everest to prove once and for all that a fully acclimatised climber, provided he moved swiftly and spent as little time as possible at extreme altitude, could climb any peak without the encumbrance of metal cylinders and a face mask. This he and Habeler did in the Spring of 1978, and for Messner the next logical extension to his theories was to dispense with the need for a partner. He would climb an Eight-thousander solo. One man, one mountain. He returned to the Diamir Flank of Nanga Parbat, where his brother had died eight years before, and tracing a new route up its formidable barriers of ice and rock, and surviving an earthquake which triggered massive avalanches below him, he achieved what was at that time his 'last great alpine dream'.

There are no indications that Massner is running out of alpine dreams. In 1979 he added K2, the world's second highest mountain, to his 'collection'. He has written more than 15 books, many of which have been translated into several languages. But he is not without his critics. Ruthlessness is one of the accusations levelled against him, commercial exploitation another. There is no doubt that Messner is a shrewd businessman, he does know how to 'market' his success but the achievements remain to speak for themselves. He is a lonely, relentless man who can be admired or criticised. He cannot be ignored.

5
Mountain Sport

Hill-walking (Plates 40, 41)

Hill-walking, or Fell-walking as it is often known in Britain, is the basic craft from which stems all mountain sport. The term covers a wide spectrum of activities ranging from an afternoon's ramble over the moors to a three-week trek to the base of a Himalayan peak. Indeed, every mountaineer must master the skills of hill-walking if only to move safely to the start of his climb while much of the upward progress on the snow and ice of a big mountain is merely an extension of basic hill-walking techniques. But most people have no desire to take the activity to these extremes—hill-walkers far exceed climbers in numbers —and to them hill-walking is an end in itself.

What does hill-walking involve? Certainly in rough and hilly country, once the skills of navigation and easy movement up-hill and down-dale are bought into play—then you're hill-walking. Scrambling, by definition clambering up technically easy rock where hand-holds are sometimes necessary but never the rope, is its upper limit. In fact the line between scrambling and easy climbing is a hazy one and its exact position depends on the individual, the weather and so forth. (See Grades in glossary.)

People have always walked the British hills but their motives were usually utilitarian until the Romantic Movement of the late eighteenth and early nineteenth centuries brought the first tourists to the hills of Snowdonia and the Lake District. The more adventurous reached the summits, often to witness the sunrise. By the 1850s the fell-walker proper had evolved—a real mountain enthusiast, frequently eccentric, who delighted in striding over the hills or scrambling up the easier rocky ridges. Some fell-walkers were pioneer alpinists who visited Wales and Cumbria in winter, alpenstocks in hand, as training for 'sterner stuff' abroad, but many were interested in exploring the British hills for their own sake. The first rock-climbers sprang from the ranks of these fell-walkers towards the end of the century and fell-walking has played its part in domestic mountaineering ever since. This is especially true in Scotland where the terrain ensures that a long mountain walk forms part of most climbing days—as indeed it does in many other parts of the world.

One notable early hill-walker was W.W. Naismith who was instrumental in founding the Scottish Mountaineering Club in 1889. Eschewing conventional transport, he would walk in a bee-line for long distances over the Highlands to attend SMC meets and in so doing he formulated what is known as Naismith's Rule: 'Allow one hour for every three miles on the map,' he declared, 'and add a further hour for every 2000 ft (600 m) of ascent.' It remains a satisfactory rule of thumb for hill-walkers even today.

Hazard in some form or another is inherent in all mountain sports and hill-walking, though least dangerous of all, is no exception. With plain common-sense, subjective accidents, such as walking over a cliff or spraining an ankle, become most unlikely. It is the objective dangers, the manifestations of the weather on rough and probably steep country, that will test the experienced and may prove deadly to the inexperienced or foolish. Rapidly changing and extreme weather is common to all high country and the experienced hill-walker should be capable not only of surviving in it and returning to his base but, ideally, of enjoying it and completing his planned expedition in safety. He should be one with the hills in all their moods. Only thus can he truly know and love them.

In Britain and Europe the hill-walker must cope with mist and rain, with electrical storms maybe, and in winter with blizzards and snow and ice as well. Mistakes may lead to nothing worse than getting lost and descending into the wrong valley but, each year, people die of hypothermia or by slipping on apparently innocent ice-sheathed hillsides. All such accidents are avoidable. Abroad, among bigger mountains, floods and river-crossings, sun and dehydration, the effects of altitude and even insects and wild animals present new hazards. But the competent hill-walker will possess the skills to move safely in such country.

The competent hill-walker should be fit enough to walk as far as he intends to go—with something in reserve: he should know his own limitations. He will be an expert navigator with map and compass and he will know something of the weather and of first-aid and simple mountain medicine. He will move safely and confidently on scree and steep ground and in winter he will be master of the ice axe and crampons that he will use. His equipment, good windproofs and proper boots for instance, will be adequate for the job in hand. Should he intend to camp or bivouac en route he will do so comfortably and cleanly. At all times he will respect the environment through which he is travelling and he will leave no permanent trace of his passing.

Perhaps the finest hill-walk in Britain is the 'Traverse of the Munros' —all 279 seperate Scottish mountains that exceed 4000 feet (1219 m). It was first completed in 1901 in a series of instalments and only in 1974 was the entire traverse made in one continuous expedition—a distance of 1639 miles (2637 km) in 112 days with no less than 449,000 feet (136,855 m) of ascent! A more practical excursion is the traverse of the 'Scottish Four-thousanders'—all seven 4000 feet (1219 m) summits—in around 50 hours. Down in England the 270 mile (435 m) Pennine Way, the Lyke Wake Walk, Offa's Dyke Path and the South Downs Way are among many less rigorous and now extremely popular long-distance walks in hill country. In Snowdonia the 'Fourteen Peaks'—the traverse of the 3000 foot (914 m) tops—is a tough and rocky walk of over 22 miles (35 km) while the 'Roof of Wales' links the Bristol Channel to the Menai Straits with 150 miles (240 km) of steep green uplands. Three really classic day trips are the Snowdon 'Horseshoe', the traverse of An Teallach in Ross and the ascent of Helvellyn in the Lake District by its famous 'Striding Edge': all three involve easy scrambling.

Once our hill-walk extends over several days and we are carrying our home on our back—then we enter the realm of the 'Back-Packer'. Many of the great mountain trails abroad do involve back-packing, although most of the fine walks in the Alps can be done from hut to hut if necessary. California's John Muir Trail along the Sierra Nevada is well known but is only part of the Pacific Crest Trail extending from Mexico to Canada. An incredible 3100 mile (5000 km) trail has recently been formulated along the entire US Continental Divide! Many people however would claim that the world's finest mountain walks are to be found in the Himalaya where the pastime is known as Trekking (Plate 41). To all intents and purposes a Trek is a Himalayan expedition but without the actual mountain climbing and amongst the most popular are those from Kathmandu to Everest Base Camp, a matter of some 18 days one way, or the circuit of the entire Annapurna massif which is done from Pokhara in some 24 days. A far cry from—and somewhat more strenuous than—an afternoon ramble over the Lakeland fells!

Fell-running (Plate 39)

Uniquely among mountain sports—at least among those outside the Communist bloc—fell-running is openly competitive. Essentially it involves racing, usually considered contrary to the very ethos of mountaineering on safety grounds if nothing else, either against the clock or among individuals or teams. Fell-running is where fell-walking, orienteering and athletics all overlap.

The sport as we know it today was born largely in the English Lake District of two parents. On the one hand there were the traditional shepherds' fell races held at village sports days in which local lads would race to the summit of a nearby fell and back again. On the other hand there was the natural inclination of the victorian fell-walkers, discussed in the last chapter, to enliven their expeditions with what might be termed 'statistical achievement'—the 'bagging' of so many tops in a given time perhaps. Ultimately the fell races attracted outsiders, both regular athletes and athletically inclined fell-walkers and mountaineers, often the very same men already interested in 'statistical achievement'.

Today fell-running has evolved into an important sport, especially popular in the north of England for obvious reasons. It embraces three distinct types of event. Firstly there is the traditional Fell Race, probably open to all comers and basically an especially steep and gruelling cross-country run over a known course with little or no navigational problems. A typical example is the Wasdale Fell Race, a circuit of the fells surrounding the valley. Famous is the Ben Nevis Race however: first run in 1895 it is now an annual event. Competitors run from Fort William to the summit of the Ben and back—4400 feet up and 4400 feet down (1340 m)—over rough stony trails or scree slopes for a total distance of some ten miles (16 km). The record stands at 87 minutes. A similar well known race in America is the Pikes Peak Marathon in Colorado in which a climb of 7500 feet (2300 m) over 26 miles (42 km) ends on a 14,000 feet (4300 m) summit! It has been won in 3 hrs 7 minutes. Probably the most popular race of this kind is Yorkshire's Three Peaks Race, traversing Pen-y-ghent, Whernside and Ingleborough in about 3 hours.

Then there are other more elaborate events which demand skilled navigation and canny route selection of which the oldest and most prestigous is the annual Vaux Mountain Trial. Here experienced competitors, starting on an interval basis, must select their own route between checkpoints on a previously unknown Lakeland course. The Karrimor Mountain Marathon is one of several two-day events and it is held in a different mountain area each year—traditionally in Norway and Switzerland. Entrants, in teams of two, are divided into a number of classes running different courses. Each team must pass scrutiny with certain obligatory equipment including a tent, stove and food, sleeping bags and foul weather and survival clothing, torch, map, compass and so forth. After a mass start a series of semi-concealed check-points must be located from map references, the night is spent at an isolated camp site under scrutiny, and the second day is like the first but leads eventually to the finish. Many teams are unable to stay the course which covers some 40–50 miles (60–80 km) and about 16 check-points over the two days. To finish at all is a worthy and not impossible achievement for a really competent yet non-athletic hill-walker, while actually to place in the event demands genuine athletic prowess, an extremely high standard of navigation, besides something of a 'feel' for mountain country, and inevitably much effort beforehand spent preparing the lightest, yet adequate, equipment. With currently nearly 2000 competitors, this race—and those similar—has given great impetus to the commercial development of efficient and safe lightweight mountain and camping gear.

Thirdly there are runs against the clock. There are so many different 'courses' all over Britain that it is not difficult to invent another and set one's own record! The classic, first established in 1905, is the 'Lake District 24 Hour Record' which seeks to traverse the greatest number of Lakeland summits in under 24 hours. If you can manage 42 tops you are entitled to belong to the exclusive Bob Graham Club, named after the man who first achieved this total in 1932. It has a current membership of 145. At the time of writing (1979) the record is held by Wasdale shepherd Joss Naylor (Plates 14, 39) with 72 peaks, a distance of 105 miles (169 km) and a climb of some 39,000 feet (12,000 m) in 23 hours 11 minutes.

Another classic is the Welsh 'Fourteen Peaks'—already mentioned in the hill-walking context. This 22 mile (36 km) expedition from the summit of Snowdon to Foel Fras in the Carneddau with 11,000 feet (3350 m) of ascent was first ambled over in 1919 in a comfortable 20 hours. This time was whittled down over the years until, in 1946, it stood at 7 hours 25. Not until mountaineers who were also international athletes appeared on the scene, men who had reconnoitred the route carefully beforehand, had located the fastest terrain and arranged for strategic changes of footwear for different ground, that 7 hours was bettered. In 1954 forty-year-old Bertie Robertson clocked just 6 hours, in 1965 Eric Beard, aged 34, made 5 hours 13 while Joss Naylor, at the age of 37 in 1973, ran the course in an astonishing 4 hrs 46 minutes. Fell-running, it seems, is not a sport for youth!

Another record is worth mentioning for although it actually involves some technical rock-climbing, it certainly also comes within the ambit of fell-running for the purpose of record breaking. The Cuillin peaks of Skye form a high horseshoe crest, gashed, gendarmed and in places knife-edged, and their traverse is the best outing of its kind in Britain. Much of the way is easy scrambling but several short sections require exposed but straight-forward rock-climbing and no less than 31 summits are crossed and over 10,000 feet (3000 m) ascended in 7 miles (11 km). First accomplished in 1911 in just over 12 hours, a competent climbing party will complete the traverse rather quicker today but in 1966 Eric Beard managed to run the ridge in just 4 hours 9 minutes.

Finally there is the Kilimanjaro–Kenya Run. The start is at 19,340 feet

(5895 m) on Africa's highest point. A descent of over 14,000 feet (4300 m) in 20 miles (32 km) leads to a waiting car and a drive of 400 miles (650 km) across the Equator to the foot of Mt Kenya. A land-rover is used to about 10,000 feet (3000 m) from where 5000 feet (1500 m) of bog and scree lead to the bottom of the final 2000 feet (600 m) rock wall. This is a serious alpine-style rock climb which even then does not end on the highest point—a descent into the icy Gate of the Mists and a further series of exposed pitches lead to Batian's 17,085 foot (5199 m) summit. The current record of just 23 hours set in 1964 is, at present, probably impossible to even challenge for political reasons. But like all athletics, and fell-running is no exception, if a record has been established, then someone, someday, will beat it!

Rock-climbing (Plates 42-8, 53, 54, 56)
Rock-climbing is the art of climbing steep rock. At its most aesthetic it has been likened to ballet in a vertical idiom. It is one of the many complementary skills that comprise 'mountaineering' although it is often practised as a sport in its own right: all mountaineers must rock-climb but the rock-climber need never set foot on a mountain, being well content with the gymnastic challenges of technical 'cragging'.

The basic technique of rock-climbing is governed by the rope—on which all safety depends. Climbers work usually in pairs, sometimes threes, and only one man will climb at a time completing a convenient distance of say 100–150 feet (30–45 m)—a pitch. His companion meanwhile remains safely attached to the rock carefully belaying the active rope. A fall by the second man, with the rope above him, is obviously not serious but a leader fall is a different matter. It was axiomatic in the days of hemp and manila ropes that 'A leader does not fall' because if he did so, for any distance, it was likely that the rope would break. Rock-climbing was a serious business and the great leaders before World War 2 were bold and resolute but never foolhardy and they deserve great respect from modern climbers. Today we use nylon ropes and running belays. With the invention of the 'nut', runners—once limited to natural spikes and flakes—can usually be placed at frequent intervals so that it is most unusual for a leader to fall far, merely twice the distance above his last point of protection—his last runner. Naturally team-work is essential for safety. Rock-climbing is no longer the high-risk sport it once was. Injuries on steep and difficult climbs are rare for hitting thin-air is painless: it is generally on the easier or more broken rock that people get hurt.

Actual progress up the rock can be by either 'free' or 'aid' techniques. Most climbs are 'free', relying entirely on natural holds, while 'aid' routes surmount blank walls and fearsome overhangs where progress otherwise is impossible. Occasional 'free' routes may require one or two points of 'aid'. Aid can be from pegs hammered into cracks or from bolts placed in drilled holes but modern ethics frown at such implements and many 'aid' routes are now completed using assistance only from cunningly placed nuts.

The bare essentials of rock-climbing equipment are a good rope and a pair of neat and well-fitting vibram soled boots. We should remember that for over 50 years all climbs were made with hemp ropes and nailed boots—or Woolworth plimsolls if they were really difficult! In 1980 however it is usual to elaborate with a pair of special PA-type lightweight rock bootees, seven or eight slings—loops of nylon webbing—and the same number of light alloy karabiners and assorted 'nuts'. Add to this a webbing climbing harness to which the rope is attached for comfort and protection in the event of a fall, and a plastic climbing helmet. In the pocket will be a climbing guide: many such little books are published, recording details of climbs made on a particular crag or area enabling the reader to locate easily the route and gain some idea of its line, its features and its difficulty. This last is expressed as a 'grade'. With such an outfit the climber should be able to complete most climbs safely although with the proliferation of modern gadgets most climbers will carry much more gear than is really necessary.

To complete his chosen climb safely and successfully the rock-climber must overcome both physical and mental problems. To follow the line of the climb as it works its way up the crag, a line that may be devious in the extreme, he will need route-finding ability. He must possess the techniques, the skills, to recognise and use each sequence of holds and so actually to carry out the series of moves that comprise the pitch. And he must break through the psychological barrier that invests the route: the nagging worry of exposure, the doubts of his own ability, the fear of falling, his apprehension of the unknown. He is exploring himself and he must make the commitment. In most cases the barrier is broken by the judgement and self-confidence generated by experience and climbing-fitness and by the placing of sound protection.

A climber's climb may be as hard or as easy as he desires. He may climb for the thrill of pushing his body and mind past their known limits or he may climb for the sheer delight of moving confidently on warm rock in impressive situations: what may extend one man—or woman—may be no challenge to the next. One of the major attractions is that, as with mountaineering in general, there are no rules to the game, only a loose code of generally accepted ethics. Climb in any way you please provided the enjoyment and expectations of other climbers is unimpaired—with riders that if a new line is beyond your ability it should be left for a better man, an existing climb should not be reduced in standard by methods not used on the first ascent and rock should not be damaged or disfigured, with pegs, bolts and so forth, unless posterity can justify it.

Man has climbed steep rock from time immemorial but until the mid-nineteenth century he usually did it for practical reasons. The St Kilda islanders, for instance, climbed difficult rock to cull the sea birds on which their economy depended while in Africa even today Masai tribesmen will climb steep and difficult crags in their quest for wild honey. But, as a sport, rock-climbing grew largely from the domestic scrambles of the early alpinists although it was the systematic series of genuine rock-climbs made in 1882 just for the fun of it around Wasdale and Langdale by the young Walter Haskett Smith—not yet an alpinist—that crystallised the game. His first ascent of Napes Needle four years later is taken as the symbolic birth of British rock-climbing.

By the turn of the century rock-climbs were being made on crags throughout all of Britain, in mountain areas and on 'outcrops' as well—particularly on the gritstone edges of the Peak District (Plate 65). In Europe the scene was similar although mountain rock-routes predominated. In America steep rock had already been climbed en route to mountain summits but the first rock-climbs per se were made by Appalachian Club members in the early 1920s on New England outcrops. Robert Underhill's 1928 ascent, in New Hampshire, of Cannon Mountain's great granite face marks the real birthday of the sport: technical climbing did not start in Yosemite until the early 1930s.

Just as there are many different crags on which to climb and many different kinds of rock to enjoy, so too are there many different manifestations of the rock-climbing game. Solo climbing is one, either with complex rope protection or entirely free. While the dangers are obvious such climbing can be a most rewarding adventure for the experienced man. Competition and Speed Climbing is another, a Russian phenomenon considered in the West to be demeaning and contrary to the very ethos of climbing. There is Big Wall Climbing when multi-day ascents, using special rope techniques and often hanging bivouacs in hammocks, are made of huge blank walls several thousand feet high. These are usually on mountains in such places as Norway and Patagonia—the notable exception being in California's beautiful Yosemite Valley where modern aid climbing was born. By contrast there are many outcrops—or 'klettergarten'—such as Harrison's Rocks near Tunbridge Wells in England or Indian Rocks at Berkeley in California, of such height, around 40 feet (12 m), that 'top-roping' is usual! Sea-cliff climbing is popular in Australia, southern France, and especially in Britain with its miles of rocky coastline. Here safety is at the crag top, often a sobering thought. In Britain such climbing has resulted in a great advance in general technical standards because seaside weather is always better than that in mountains and hard climbing can take place all year round. In recent years exploratory climbers have rediscovered the excitement of the sea-cliff traverse in which easy ways down to the sea are linked along the sea cliffs where escape upwards is very hard or impossible (Plates 42–4). Superb expeditions have resulted, many of great length and enlivened by such rope manoeuvres as pendules and tyrolean traverses to escape a ducking in inhospitable seas. Ascents are made too of Sea Stacks, isolated pinnacles such as Balls Pyramid (1800 ft/549 m) in the Tasman Sea or the Old Man of Hoy (450 ft/140 m) off Orkney (Plate 43). And to descend perhaps from the sublime to the ridiculous 'climbing walls' have been built in the gymnasiums and sports halls of many cities. Regular training in such unaesthetic situations has again resulted in an upsurge of technical expertise, so much so in fact that without regular training the hardest rock climbs are no longer possible! Yes indeed, there is something to climb everywhere!

Ice Climbing (Plates 49-52, 59, 60, 65)

Like rock climbing, ice climbing is another skill essential to the complete mountaineer: much we have read of rock climbing applies equally here. Unlike rock climbing however, its very nature demands either high mountains themselves or winter conditions in mountainous country and its exponents have almost invariably been mountaineers— although in Scotland not necessarily alpine mountaineers.

We can distinguish three overlapping facets to the game. First there is alpine ice climbing where ice, rather than rock, provides the route to a mountain summit. Although this comes within the ambit of our alpine climbing chapter, the great ice faces are important in our context. In the European Alps such faces may reach 3000 feet (1000 m) in height but because of their glacial nature they are unlikely to exceed 60° in steepness except for short distances: where thin ice pours over steeper rock bands or mixed ground for instance, where the face funnels into a couloir perhaps or where glacial obstacles such as 'schrunds or seracs occur. Such features change from year to year. In good conditions with a covering of hard-frozen snow the problems presented by such faces, apart from the short steep sections, include an objective danger—stone fall for instance—and a psychological one of exposure in the middle of a vast, smooth, white wall. Technically the climbing is not difficult. In winter, however, conditions change. Rock may be plated with ice and many steep couloirs which are summer death-traps have recently been discovered to provide grand ice climbs of Scottish format. Short but very steep ice problems occur also in glacier ice-falls but this is more likely in the really great ranges such as the Himalaya (eg. Everest's Khumbu Ice-fall).

Secondly we should consider Scottish winter climbing of which the late great Tom Patey wrote: '. . . to describe Scottish Winter Climbing merely in terms of training for (so-called) Greater Mountaineering . . . would be heresy. The Scottish brand of winter mountaineering is unique!' Scotland's mountains, though relatively small and holding no permanent snow, are often remote and craggy and during the long winter months an everlasting succession of blizzard, thaw, frost and wind creates snow and ice conditions worthy of far greater and higher peaks. To venture safely into the Scottish mountains in winter is genuinely to 'mountaineer'. When the SMC was founded in 1889 one of its original objectives was to promote winter mountaineering and this has been the most important aspect of Scottish climbing ever since. With notable exceptions ice climbing started in much the same way as rock-climbing—in the gullies where exposure was at a minimum. Bulges of water-ice and icicle-draped chimneys alternated with verglassed rock-steps and led to a steep snowy head-wall complete with overhanging cornice. Unfortunately, until they are of a high degree of difficulty, gullies tend to have a peculiar sameness. Soon climbers ventured out onto ice-plastered ridges and later onto buttresses and faces, always meanwhile attempting harder and harder gullies and ice-runnels and other natural ice traps which have always provided the foundation of the sport. Forcing routes up rock radically altered by a temporary carapace of snow and ice is the essence of Scottish winter climbing.

The third facet is largely a recent North American phenomenon owing much of its inspiration to Scottish experiences and—in Canada— actually to emigré Scots climbers. In winter the waterfalls and cascades of the mountain states and New England freeze solid creating pillars and chutes of hard water-ice sometimes as high as 1000 feet (300 m) with long vertical sections and occasional overhanging bulges. Climbs on such giant icicles are as bold as they are spectacular and have only been made possible by recent radical advances in equipment and techniques.

How is it done? The basic system of roped climbing is essentially the same as on rock except on the great ice faces where certain alpine systems will apply. Upward progress is made using crampons and ice axe and, when possible, the rock techniques of bridging, jamming, chimneying and so forth. Away from the big alpine faces ice is rarely smooth and flat! Belays are taken, preferably on rock with nuts or pegs but otherwise on ice-screws, dead-men, snow-stakes or even ice-bollards, while

125

protection is arranged in the same way.

Wearing nailed boots the early ice-climbers hacked a ladder of steps using long and heavy axes. The method applied equally to the Alps, to Scotland and to icy mountains everywhere. With the advent of the crampon steeper ice was climbed and smaller steps sufficed. Once 'vibram' boots arrived crampons became essential and using the flat-footed French 'pied a plat' technique—actually developed by English-man Oscar Eckenstein—and support from a now lighter axe, slopes of up to 50° could be cramponed before steps were cut. The next inovation was the 12-point crampon with two forward pointing claws. The tech-nique, an Austrian one but known as 'pied en avant', was to kick directly into the ice with just the front points. Although much steeper ice could be cramponed proper handholds were necessary and, as the angle became really steep, tiny foot-nicks were used with larger steps in which to rest. Hand-holds were provided by daggers or by the axe pick used in the same way—with usually one tool in each hand—and on very steep Scottish ice by cut finger holds. For these methods rigid boots were essential and many climbers preferred rigid crampons as well rather than the centrally hinged models which were more comfortable on easy slopes.

Then it was the turn of the axe itself. Early on the Scots had developed very short axes, easier to handle when cutting on vertical ice. Now the geometry of the axe was to be tailored to climb rather than to cut. The American Chouinard axe with its graceful yet deeply curved pick appeared followed by its derivations, the very short Chouinard alpine hammer and the Climaxe. In Scotland Hamish MacInnes produced the Terrordactyl, an all metal tool with a straight pick dropped steeply at 55° to the shaft. Other designers followed suit on the same principles and a proliferation of ice-tools is available today. Which to use is a personal preference but generally speaking 'curved' gear is easier to use on alpine terrain but requires great arm strength on the steepest ground while 'dropped' gear performs well on poor ice, verglas or even rock holds and on steep ice is less tiring for weaker-armed climbers. Armed with a pair of such tools and rigid crampons, vertical and even bulging ice is climbed swiftly and without cutting a step. The points of both picks are hooked into the ice above the head with a light blow and, with three-point contact supporting his weight, the climber moves up one foot or hand at a time. On such steepness the technique is exacting but stretches of 30 feet (10 m) can be climbed quickly between resting places and on ice of easier angle great speed can be maintained, relaxed and with security, for long periods.

Naturally an experienced ice-climber develops his own variations to these methods—there are no rules. But one of his tools will have a hammer head and both will sit comfortably in holsters at his waist when not in use. Besides his ice and rock pegs, karabiners, slings and maybe dead-men, he may carry a small file to hone his crampons and axe points to optimum sharpness and perhaps a light alloy snow-shovel—to dig out stances, carve a snow-cave or excavate an avalanche should the worst happen—even to surmount deep and horrible snow. And of course his clothing will reflect the weather and the possibility of really cold emergencies. At his finger tips will be all the usual rock and rope techniques as well as such specialist snow and ice techniques as self-arrest with the ice axe, glissading and the New Zealand foot-brake. Ethical considerations will trouble him little for ice and snow are ephemeral things and in winter no holds are barred except that it is not considered good form to cut a route which more competent climbers can crampon. But on the winter mountains he is free, freer even than in summer because the world is his alone and his footsteps, like those of yesterday, will be gone tomorrow.

Ski Mountaineering (Plate 8)
A cynical journalist once described skiing as, 'superficial thrill-seeking on boards . . . the yo-yo sport'. He was blinkered of course by the popular image of skiing as a social winter holiday or an exciting TV spectator sport. The mountaineer, by contrast, regards skiing in a more practical light as a means of transport over snow-covered terrain. According to an old Scandinavian tradition the first ski were bed boards strapped by an irate wife to her feet to pursue her offending husband across the snowy fields. It is said that she soon caught him. What could be more practical than that?

There are two basic styles of skiing, Nordic and Alpine. Certainly ski of sorts were used in Norway 4000 years ago but it was not until the 1850s that one Sondre Norheim invented heel bindings and contrived the Telemark and Christiania turns to manoeuvre on the steeper slopes. A ski school opened in Oslo in 1882 and competive cross-country racing and ski-jumping followed. The first Briton to learn the art was probably W.C. Slingsby at about that time.

Nordic skiing—'langlauf' or 'cross-country' as it is also known—is the natural Scandinavian style and it developed in a hilly as opposed to a mountainous landscape. While it has become recreational there is nothing superficial about it. The equipment used is simple and light: long slender wooden ski are carefully waxed to glide and yet grip, straightforward binding systems hold only the toes of supple slipper-like boots whose heels rise completely free, poles are long and whippy bamboos. The technique is astonishingly dynamic and graceful and a good nordic skier can cover great distances, up, down and along, effortlessly and at a runner's pace. Modern developments have made life easier and widened the scope of the system to cover more difficult terrain. Plastic ski with steel edges have appeared for use on hard or icy slopes, 'fish-scale' and 'mica-base' soles obviate the mystical art of waxing while fibreglass poles are stronger and more springy than bamboo. Nordic skiing has become extremely popular in America in recent years and promises to become so in Europe and Britain—often as an escape from people, lift-queues and commercialism. But its application to the winter fell-walker and mountaineer is obvious.

Skiing spread to the Alps towards the turn of the century where Arnold Lunn, a notable mountaineer, did much to shape its popularity as a sport prior to 1914. The alpine terrain is more rugged and precipitous and the slopes higher and more icy than in Norway and 'Alpine' techniques and equipment have evolved to cope with it and the requirements of the developing 'downhill only' sport. Lunn was a pioneer of ski-touring and ski-mountaineering which are basically the same thing : the former embracing high level ski journeys over passes and glaciers, the latter seeking summits as well. He made the first ski ascents of such large peaks as the Dom (14,911 ft/4544 m), the Weisshorn and the Eiger.

The ski-mountaineer must master the skills of the winter alpinist, particularly his knowledge of snow, avalanche and glacier travel, besides those of the 'downhill' skier, being able to turn strongly off piste and—ideally—to ski parallel. The ski he uses are similar to regular 'downhill' ski but more flexible, his boots are high and stiff mountaineering boots adapted to accept ski bindings and usually with clips which can instantly lock the ankle for descents. He uses the normal metal poles. The bindings are of crucial importance for the foot must flex and the heel rise for level and uphill travel while the entire boot must be imobilised for downhill skiing. A safety release must also be incorporated. The result is a 'dual purpose' step-in binding although many skiers, especially in America, still favour lighter cable bindings. For climbing 'skins' are quickly clipped or waxed onto the underside of the ski. Originally seal skin, these are long strips of plush with backward facing hair. On steep slopes 'harscheisen', little metal teeth, can be slid beneath the boot as a sort of crampon. Under his jacket he will carry a tiny radio gadget of the Autophon or Pieps type which should enable his companions to locate him rapidly should he be overwhelmed by an avalanche. Once the rhythmic relaxed technique of 'skinning' is learnt, uphill progress becomes suprisingly swift and easy although downhill running with a large rucksack in deep snow is a strenuous business. Few experiences can be more delightful than watching one's ski tips breaking virgin snow across a high snowfield.

Which style to use? Experienced ski-mountaineers today often combine the techniques and equipment of both to suit their ambitions and requirements. There are no rules. The limitations of Alpine ski are their weight and complexity but they will be favourite in steep and rugged high mountain country where ice will be encountered and glaciers crossed and they are extremely controllable in hazardous situations such as craggy slopes and ice-falls. Nordic ski on the other hand are ideal for gentler terrain, for rolling or flat wilderness country, for winter back-packing for instance, where their lightness is an advantage and their inherent inability to turn tightly and quickly presents no problems. With steel edges and cabled heel bindings—say 'Silvretta' or 'Kandahar' type—basically Nordic gear is suitable for touring in more rugged mountain terrain. Ski of some kind are essential for approaching alpine climbs in winter and best are those easiest to collect afterwards from the bottom of the climb!

Ski touring can be enjoyed in Britain. The Scottish Cairngorms especially provide excellent terrain and good conditions often persist into late May. The linking of the four 'Four Thousanders' on alpine or nordic touring ski is a notable expedition and at its best such skiing can be far more atmospheric—because of the subtle colours and the lower sun—than anything in the Alps. The complete crossing of the Highlands from sea to sea, a tough 140 miles (230 km) nordic expedition from Fort William to Stonehaven, still remains uncompleted although a much shorter crossing has been made further north in Sutherland. Good touring is possible, when conditions permit, in the Lake District, the Pennines and elsewhere.

The most famous ski tour in the world is the Haute Route. Linking Chamonix to Saas Fee via Zermatt and eleven high glacier passes along the crest of the Pennine Alps, this 80 mile (130 km) traverse was first skied in 1911 by a party led by Marcel Kurz, the great pioneer of ski mountaineering. Today the expedition is very popular; it is usually completed in spring, on alpine ski, going from hut to hut, in about ten days. It has been done in 24 hours! With their long glaciers and high passes the Bernese Alps are also prime touring terrain and the entire length of the Alps, from Austria to the French Maritimes, has been skied several times taking around 50 days. Other regions notable for ski touring—either alpine or nordic—include Norway and Arctic Lapland, the Pyrenees, the Atlas, the peaks of Corsica, the California Sierra and India's Kulu Himalaya. Ski have been used on Kenya's little Lewis Glacier and even on Uganda's Stanley Ice Plateau! Surprisingly expeditionary mountaineers have seemed reluctant to use ski on really large mountains where they could be extremely useful. Members of the 1952 Swiss Everest Expedition skied down the horrendous Khumbu Ice-fall postmonsoon and the 1971 International Everest Expedition, trapped by storm for ten days high in the Western Cwm, could well have escaped on ski and subsequently returned fit to reach the summit. Without doubt the ability to cross snow-covered mountain country on ski is an essential skill for the all-round mountaineer.

Alpine Climbing (Plates 52-9, 64, 65)

Alpine Climbing is a style—a concept even—rather than a definite set of techniques. The birthplace of mountaineering as a sport was the European Alps where hundreds of summits, most of them carrying snow, ice and glaciers to some extent, rise above 10,000 feet (3000 m). The French coined the term 'alpinism', now universally adopted, to describe climbing that sort of mountain, anywhere in the world, in the style developed in that Range. The basic techniques of rock and ice climbing that we have already examined still apply but they are indulged in a new environment and under new constraints. The Alpine Concept is now even being applied among the highest mountains of the world, mountains twice the size of the European Alps, in direct contrast to the expeditionary 'siege tactics' previously considered essential. What is this style and how did it develop?

By 1865—the end of the 'Golden Age'—mountaineering, far from being an eccentric diversion, had emerged as a recognizable sport and the men who made it so were largely British. They were men of education though not necessarily of great substance and they sprung from similar professional, academic or ecclesiastical backgrounds. They were very much a product of the social and economic circumstances of Victorian Britain. They were great and speedy walkers, these men, and starting from, say, a comfortable inn in a village such as Zermatt, it was not difficult for them to climb even the highest peaks and return for dinner the following day. One night would be spent in a convenient bivouac.

It was usual in those days to employ one or more guides and perhaps a porter or two, the latter to carry the victuals, blankets and firewood. The guides themselves, originally local peasants or hunters, soon became a corps d'elite of skilled craftsmen, developing a proud tradition of comradeship and team-work with their employers. It was a relationship which reached its peak at the turn of the century with such teams as Ryan and the Lochmatters or Young and Knubel, but it was to disappear as guideless climbing became the norm. There were then as now, great guides and merely competent guides, and it is fashionable in the alpine countries today for the best amateurs to take the rigorous guides' qualifying examinations.

In 1868 the Swiss Alpine Club built the first climbing hut on the Matterhorn and by 1880 there were no less than 34 huts at high and strategic sites in the Swiss Alps alone. The traditional bivouac had become obsolete. Today there are more than 700 huts scattered throughout the Alps ranging from elaborate structures offering restaurant service and accommodation for 100 to tiny 'bivis' with scant room for four. It would be fair to claim that there is no classic route of moderate difficulty in the Alps that necessitates a bivouac under normal conditions. Conditions however are not always normal and many harder climbs do require one—or more—bivouacs. They form a part of 'alpine style', as does speed which is still a primary consideration of all alpine climbing. Speed is safety where weather is never guaranteed and where objective dangers, rockfall, wet snow and avalanches for instance, are expected hazards.

A typical scenario for a climb of moderate difficulty in the Alps might be as follows:

In promising weather two or maybe three alpinists will set out from the valley where they have been lodging or camping to reach the hut convenient to their chosen climb. The walk, of several hours, may be long and steep but up-hill transport—a cable car for instance—may be available for part of it at a price. Their rucksacks, designed for climbing rather than for big loads, will carry nothing superfluous. Climbing gear, a minimum of survival gear, an evening meal and snacks for the climb and almost certainly in the Alps an excellent local map and pocket guide-book detailing their climb and others on the mountain will be packed. Arriving at the hut in the late afternoon they will make the guardian's acquaintance, giving him their meal—say soup and pasta— to cook for a fee. Wealthy visitors might buy a full dinner complete with wine while less fortunate folk may be allowed to cook for themselves on their own stoves in a special outhouse. The guardian might advise on current conditions and on their route and on weather prospects. But huts are expensive and often crowded and some modern climbers prefer to avoid them, recapturing something of the original atmosphere with a bivouac nearer the climb. The hut rule will be early to bed because, depending on the climb, a start will be made anywhere between midnight and first light. After a perfunctory breakfast the climbers will set off by torch-light aiming to reach the first difficult ground with the dawn.

Once on the climb the climbers will probably remain unroped—for speed—as long as they consider it safe to do so. Once roped they may decide to move singly, pitch-by-pitch with proper belays—safe but slow, or to move together on a short rope in 'alpine style' which is faster but less secure. Except on glaciers many experienced alpinists prefer to remain unroped until difficulty forces them to move singly and this is fastest of all. A compromise is reached between protection and speed. Many tyro alpinists are caught in storms or forced to bivouac by slowness resulting from excessive caution and excessive loads of— usually—emergency clothing!

Eventually the summit is reached. It may be mid-morning or it could already be late afternoon. Usually descent will be down an easier route —possibly the 'voie normale', or by rappel down steep rock. If the mountain is popular the snow will be pisted and patient guides may still be shepherding down their charges. But the sun may be hot, the snow soft, the glacier dangerous and the climbers weary. Many accidents occur on the descent. Sooner or later they reach the hut again, or another one, with plans for the next climb or they may descend to the valley to enjoy a good meal and a bottle of wine.

Hut systems, of course, exist in only a few other alpine ranges, notably in New Zealand and East Africa, and although expeditionary strategy may be necessary to reach many alpine peaks, the tactics of actually climbing them, and the equipment needed, will always be similar. The normal rock, snow and ice gear we have discussed previously is used, with the ice axe being the crucial tool. Alpine boots are substantial and not light and helmets are worn, more as a protection against rock fall than anything else while warm clothing is essential— for temperatures at altitude drop well below freezing at night and in the shade. Climbing on doubled 9 mm rope is favoured to allow for long rappels. On the more difficult and lengthy routes where planned bivouacs are necessary a down jacket and/or lightweight sleeping bag is carried often with a light pole-less nylon tent or 'bivi-sack' and a small gas stove for brewing-up.

Thus Alpine Climbing emerges as the concept of moving fast and light over rock, snow and ice or mixed ground on fairly large glaciated mountains. Because of the length of the climbs and the height of the peaks the alpinist himself requires stamina, fitness and route-finding ability besides mastery of all the techniques of his craft. Alpine Climbing is committing, it is not a low-risk sport, objective dangers are omnipresent and it demands of him a singleness of purpose he is unlikely to have needed on smaller mountains. In short the alpinist must be a real mountaineer.

Expeditioning (Plates 58, 59, 61-65)

Few other mountains of comparable size are as accessible as the European Alps. Usually such mountains are more or less remote and an overland journey of some kind is necessary to reach them. The Oxford Dictionary defines an Expedition as a journey for a specific purpose, but this is a vague definition as early climbers referred to any trip above the snowline as an 'expedition' while today the term is often used to describe an especially long climb, particularly one of a traversing nature such as the Cuillin Ridge of Skye. Expeditionary Mountaineering is understood to mean climbing on mountains, usually but not necessarily large ones, which require a long journey to reach. The climbs themselves may be alpine or at high altitude or on very small mountains —it is the fact that they are remote that is important.

While the journey is only a means to an end, it is nevertheless important, for both the expedition members and their equipment must be in a fit state, on its completion, to climb the mountain they have come so far to reach. Wise leaders will plan the journey to be something of a holiday if possible, a period of relaxation after the inevitable frenzy of departure and before the ordeals of climbing commence. Often the journey is made on foot—hence the term 'approach march'—but the nature of the terrain and its inhabitants, if any, may dictate other methods. In Alaska and nothern Canada it is usual to fly into the mountains and local bush-pilots have become especially skilled at landing their light aircraft with ski on high glaciers or with floats on remote lakes. In Nepal STOL planes are sometimes used to reduce three week approach marches to a few days, while Russians use helicopters to reach their Pamir and Tien Shan base-camps. Particularly in the polar regions supplies may be air-dropped. When mountains rise close to the sea, as in Greenland and Norway, boats may provide the only access. Except on the approaches to the Tibesti and Hoggar ranges of the Sahara, expeditions are unlikely to use motor vehicles: not only would their use probably be logistically unsound but once off designated roads it would almost certainly be forbidden—quite rightly—for a wide range of environmental reasons.

The great advantage of walking in to a base camp is that it is a good way to get fit and gradually to acclimatise to altitude, besides usually being a really enjoyable experience, but food and equipment will need transporting by local porters or pack-animals. The former can be a mixed blessing, but they may be friendly, loyal and utterly reliable and give a fair day's work for a good day's pay (Plates 10, 13, 15). In Nepal, in 1980, a porter's official wage was nearly £1 per day, far above the average national income. A good porter, well led, will carry almost anywhere that two feet will take him—or her—and cope happily with snow-slopes and rock scrambles. Alternatively porters may be troublesome and entirely destroy an expedition with strikes, theft and restrictive practices. In recent years this has been a common occurrence in the Karakorum where wages are nearly three times the Nepalese rate and labour relations are notoriously tempestuous. Other ranges where porters are often used include those of East and Central Africa, especially in the Ruwenzori where lengthy operations without their assistance are impracticable.

Pack-animals may be the only means of transport or a cheaper alternative to porters. While carrying considerably more than a man, they are not as flexible and are useless on really awkward ground. Typically llamas or mules are used in the Andes, yaks in the Himalaya (Plate 11), goats and sheep in parts of northern India and pack-horses in the Rocky Mountains. Some small expeditions attempt to carry all their own supplies and, while this is a commendable idea when the journey itself is the goal, it is bound to restrict any climbing objectives even in inhabited regions where adequate food can be purchased locally. A Nepali porter will normally carry some 70 lbs (30 kg) and it is unrealistic to expect expedition members to carry any more than this regularly.

The size and complexity of expeditions has always aroused controversy but modern opinion is that 'small is beautiful'. There is much truth in Tilman's old adage that, if an expedition couldn't be organised on the back of an envelope, then it was not an expedition but a military operation! Certainly small competent teams can be fast moving, highly successful, inexpensive and—most important—have great fun, but a certain minimum of preparation is essential if things are to run smoothly and safely. Participants must be carefully selected, food and equipment thoughtfully chosen and the miles of red tape which nowadays festoon most expeditionary mountains meticulously coiled up. An accident or medical emergency in any remote area is a very serious business and as rescue must be assumed to be out of the question, the expedition must be prepared, and insured, for any such eventuality. This factor will be considered in any mountaineering decisions. A small expedition does require a major personal commitment from its members.

Large expeditions, on the other hand, are usually unnecessary, often cumbersome, always grossly expensive and sometimes unhappy. Irresponsibly they may also disrupt a fragile wilderness environment and a local subsistence economy when, for instance, they denude an area of its sparse timber resources for firewood and hire large numbers of porters during the corn-planting season. They can't make hundred-rupee notes into chapattis! No longer does the end justify the means, the style of the expedition is now all important. Perhaps such huge expeditions as the unsuccessful French attempt on K2's SSW Ridge in 1979, with its 23 climbers, 1450 porters and hang-gliders, are the last of the dinosaurs?

Expeditioning and the exploration, either original or personal, which must be associated with it, has always been an integral part of the concept of mountaineering. For those who practice it, who penetrate remote and wilderness country and who, self-reliant, locate, reconnoitre and climb small peaks or the ultimate mountains, there can be no greater satisfaction.

High Altitude Mountaineering (Pates 66-71)

This section is about climbing really big mountains. At around 18,000 feet (5500 m) mountaineering starts to become a very different proposition to what it is below. The term 'high altitude' is relative: its effects are certainly apparent at 15,000 feet (4500 m) on Mont Blanc, while the Caucasus—where three peaks top 17,000 feet (5200 m)—is merely 'super-alpine'. Perhaps because of their equatorial situation, stable weather and straightforward access, only the higher peaks of the Peruvian Andes—the 20 or so above 20,000 feet (6000 m)—can be considered true high altitude mountains, yet Mount McKinley (20,322 ft/ 6194 m) and Mount Logan (19,520 ft/5951 m), both huge and remote mountains at high latitudes, definitely belong in the high altitude league.

Inevitably high altitude mountaineering is expeditionary, lengthy approaches are usual and remoteness is the norm. Merely to establish a base camp demands the skills of successful expeditioning. Base camp will be home throughout the expedition. It will be from here that local porters are paid off, pack-animals sent down or aircraft asked to come back later, and it is always tempting to site such a camp as high as possible. But high altitude climbing is rigorous, both physically and mentally, and base camp should be located as a 'rest-home' rather than a front line 'dug-out'. Now the business of climbing can actually begin.

The actual strategy of the ascent will have been decided at an early stage of planning: three different tactics—or even a combination of them—can be chosen. Most commonly used are *siege tactics*. By repeated attempts over a period of time the climbers will place a series of camps higher and higher up the mountain, linking each by a well marked route with ropes fixed over difficult sections as necessary, and each—once the route is established—just a short day's climb apart. The climbers take it in turn to break new ground while their companions ferry loads, improve the route or rest. Men, food and equipment should flow smoothly up the mountain until a camp can be placed sufficiently near the top for a summit bid to be mounted from it. Should the first attempt fail, a second rope of climbers who will have moved up in support will make another attempt—and so on until the mountain is climbed or the expedition admits defeat. Most expeditions will hope to mount several successful attempts and place as many members as possible on the summit, but even if one man has succeeded, he has done so on the shoulders of his companions and the whole expedition is successful. This style of climbing is very much a team effort.

The advantages of such tactics are apparent safety and security. In the event of a storm or an accident retreat is assured and the climbers in each camp are mutually supporting. The expedition can slog away at the mountain, with fresh men in front and exhausted men resting at base camp, until it is climbed. But the disadvantages are those of the typically big expeditions who practice siege tactics. To be effective, adequate men, equipment, time and money—and planning—are essential. Siege tactics are extremely vulnerable to breakdowns in communications, due to weather, sickness or radio failure, or to morale which is easily upset when progress is slow and much load-carrying is involved. Efficient logistics are crucial and the problem presented is a pyramidical one: as the route reaches higher and higher so more and more men, tents and supplies must be committed at each level on the mountain just to support the two men out in front. For this reason most expeditions in the Himalaya and the Karakorum rely heavily on the assitance of high-altitude porters, almost invariably sherpas and hunza respectively. Some sherpas claim, not without cause, that certain less-strong expeditions, particularly on Everest, have '. . . been carried to success on our shoulders.' Far more commendable, and very much the way of the future, are recent attempts on Everest and Himalchuli—another very large mountain—by small New Zealand and British parties without any sherpa assistance whatsoever, the climbers doing all their own carrying, albeit unsuccessfully.

An alternative, and a very viable one on peaks up to about 23,000 feet (7000 m) is to use more or less *alpine tactics*. While still possible, such tactics on larger mountains demand very powerful and confident climbers. Careful acclimatisation before the attempt is important and several reconnaissances on the route itself or on surrounding viewpoints from which it can be studied will probably be made to this end. It is likely that at least one camp will be placed above base camp before the climbers break into true alpine style on their bid for the summit during which they will move fast, be light and self-contained, and bivouac when necessary. Obviously several variations on the theme are possible, one is to use sherpa assistance to establish, and stock, whatever camps are placed, another is to use fixed ropes and permanent bivouacs—snow caves for instance—as insurance against bad weather and the descent. A four man Anglo-French team climbed Kangchenjunga by a new route using just these tactics in 1979. The advantages are those of simplicity: alpine tactics require a minimum of climbers, equipment and 'hassle' and they are relatively inexpensive. The very disadvantages—total commitment, loneliness and vulnerability—are attractions to many experienced mountaineers. But a long sequence of consecutive bivouacs at high altitude, sometimes as many as ten, are physically extremely demanding and progress, or indeed the descent, can be a fight for survival. Arguably there is less to go wrong with alpine tactics, but if they do the penalties are severe!

A third tactic admits some interesting possibilities. *Capsule tactics* feature something of both previous systems but have been little used to date. The concept is that four or six climbers, say, operate from one relatively comfortable and well provisioned camp which is gradually moved up the mountain, higher and higher. While one rope is pushing the route forward above camp and fixing ropes, their companions are moving up the gear from the previous site and eventually removing the fixed ropes below. It is a system which owes much to Yosemite principles of Big Wall Climbing. Retreat is cut but support is available and a safe haven is on hand when the weather turns bad. Ideally an easier and quicker descent route should be chosen from the summit. The classic example of the success of Capsule Tactics was in 1965 when six Americans spent 37 days, shifted camp 11 times and ascended 12,6000 feet (3800 m) to make the first ascent of Mount Logan's six mile ($9\frac{1}{2}$ km) long Hummingbird Ridge.

But there is more to high altitude climbing than just the tactics employed. The single most important consideration is the effect of high altitude on the climber himself. Symptoms may occur as low as 8000 feet (2500 m) and be ignored, but to do so ten thousand feet higher can lead to disaster. The worst effects of the oxygen depleted atmosphere at high altitude, as the climber feels them, are shortness of breath which renders all work, all progress, an incredible effort, and altitude sickness in its various forms—one of which, pulmonary oedema, can be rapidly fatal. Other associated effects are insomnia, lack of appetite, dehydration, susceptibility to frostbite and so forth, often coupled with a change of personality and defects of judgement. To counter these effects, indeed to exist at all, necessitates proper acclimatisation. This means a gradual ascent, in easy stages, from 10,000 feet (3000 m) upwards, with plenty of rest and no undue exertion: a good maxim is to climb high and sleep low. While acclimatisation continues, fitness deteriorates above about 20,000 feet (6000 m) and it seems impossible to recuperate—or to throw off a minor cold for instance—without descending well below this level. The effects of altitude vary, in both kind and degree, from person to person.

The use of oxygen for high altitude mountaineering has always been controversial. It has usually been considered necessary, or at least desirable, when attempting summits above 25,000 feet (7500 m) or so, but now that all four of the world's highest summits have been reached without its use there are strong ethical reasons against its continued employment except on difficult new routes and for medical emergencies. It is in any case expensive and heavy.

Other considerations tend to be those normally associated with alpine climbing and expeditioning but exacerbated by the size and height of the mountain. Food is naturally important when altitude affects appetite and fitness must be maintained over a long period. A liquid intake of about a gallon a day is necessary, not easy when all water must be melted from snow. Good communications can be critical and most siege expeditions in the Himalaya use walkie-talkie radios. Special clothing, boots, sleeping bags and tents designed to withstand extreme cold and strong winds are needed. And decisions must be taken about the weather: in the Himalaya, for instance, there are two seasons, pre- and post-monsoon, the former with less stable weather, the latter with colder and windier conditions. When best should the climb be attempted?

At one time few high altitude climbs were technically difficult—most would have been considered little more than a 'snow plod' in the Alps. But now that all the world's highest summits have been reached, the accent has turned to new more interesting and thus more difficult routes. The 1970s saw entirely new standards being reached and high altitude climbs almost as hard as any in the Alps have been successfully attempted. Undoubtedly the happy hunting grounds of the future—for the really enterprising mountaineer—lie among the higher peaks of the world.

History of Mountaineering at a Glance

The history of mountaineering is reflected by developments and trends in Europe and, in recent years, in America. Events in the Alps, that crucible of world mountaineering, not only influence events and achievements among the Greater Ranges and in non-alpine countries, but are themselves influenced by happenings elsewhere, particularly in Britain. Rarely does mountaineering develop in complete isolation.

While these tables are bound to be highly selective—and indeed controversial—and while they ignore completely mountaineering in other important areas, they will demonstrate how mountaineering has evolved along three of its most indicative and influential major axes.

The first column indicates a related event elsewhere.

		United Kingdom
Alps ⟵—————⟶	1857	The Alpine Club is founded: its early members scramble in the British hills in winter.
	1882	Haskett Smith begins his systematic series of rock-climbs in the Lake District, climbing just for fun.
	1883	In Snowdonia the daunting N. Face of Lliwedd is climbed by two members of the 'Society of Welsh Rabbits'
	1886	Haskett Smith makes first ascent of Napes Needle: it marks the beginning of rock-climbing as a sport.
	1889	The Scottish Mountaineering Club is founded, its forerunner, the old 'Gaiter Club', was founded in 1849. The SMC is the first 'domestic' mountaineering club.
Alps 1870 —————⟶	1894	Haskett Smith publishes 'Climbing in the British Isles'—the first technical descriptions of British rock-climbs. Norman Collie makes the first ascent of Tower Ridge on Ben Nevis: the beginning of real climbing in Scotland.
	1898	Raeburn's ascent of the gully that bears his name on Lochnagar marks the beginning of

139

		difficult Scottish winter climbing.
		The Climbers Club is founded and crystallises the development of Welsh rock-climbing.
	early 1900s	Rubber soled plimsolls are introduced for the most difficult rock climbs.
Alps 1871 ────────▶	1907	Ladies Alpine Club founded—the world's first ladies mountaineering club.
Alps 1881 ────────▶	1909	The C.C. publishes the first 'pocket' climbing guide of modern format to British rock: 'Climbs on Lliwedd' by Archer Thompson and Andrews.
Alps 1868 ────────▶	1912	The Rucksack Club opens the first climbing hut in Britain at Cwm Eigiau in Snowdonia.
	1914	Herford's ascent of the formidable Central Buttress on Scafell is a landmark in the development of British rock-climbing. Even today it is an important route.
	1927	Fred Pigott's team force the first line up the E. Buttress of Clogwyn Du'r Arddu— hitherto considered inviolate: it is a major breakthrough, the first climb on Snowdonia's major cliff.
Himalaya 1931 ◀───	1928	Jack Longland's team consolidate the breakthrough with the first route on 'Cloggy's' W. Buttress. It includes Frank Smythe.
	1930s	Outcrop climbing develops apace in the Pennines and elsewhere: changing social conditions and patterns of leisure popularise rock-climbing in areas accessible to the great cities of the north.
	1937	Bill Murray develops the slater's pick into a short ice-climbing tool. In Glencoe Murray and Mackenzie climb Crowberry Ridge by the Garrick Shelf—it is the prototype of the modern ice climb.
	1944	The British Mountaineering Council is formed: it is Winthrop Young's idea that British climbing should have a central voice.
Alps 1947 ◀─────── Himalaya 1951 ◀──	1947	British climbers return to the Alps after an absence of 8 years.
	late 1940s	Changing social conditions and increased mobility make climbing a 'mass sport': Britain's mountain areas are now accessible

to all at holidays and weekends.
Nylon ropes become available for the first
time and by the early 1950s their use is
universal. The axiom that 'a leader does not
fall' is soon forgotten.

Alps 1935 ⟶ | 1950 | Bourdillon and Nicol climb the N. Face of
the Dru: it marks the British return to high
standard alpinism after more than two
decades.

Alps mid 1930s ⟶ | early 1950s | Vibram soles come into general use in
Britain.

| 1951 | Joe Brown and Don Whillans begin their
partnership, the most powerful ever in
British climbing—which they dominate for a
decade. Three years of unprecedented
development follow and British free rock-
climbing standards lead the world.

Alps 1933 ⟶ | | First British ascent Cima Grande N. Face.

| 1952 | Brown and Whillans climb Cenotaph Corner.
A landmark.

Alps 1954 ← | 1953 | The elitist Alpine Climbing Group is formed
Himalaya 1956 ← | | to encourage top class alpinism among
British climbers.

Alps 1954 ← | 1954 | British alpinists return to 'world class'.

| 1950s | Limestone crags are explored seriously for
the first time and discovered not to be as
loose as expected. The 'Limestone Revolu-
tion' follows.

Alps 1937 ⟶ | 1955 | First British ascent Piz Badile N.E. Face.
Alps 1951 ⟶ | | First British ascent Grand Capucin E. Face.

| 1957 | BMC estimates there are 18,000 'climbers'
in UK.

Alps early 1950s ⟶ | late 1950s | 'Duvets'—down jackets and 'pieds
d'elephant' are first brought home by British
alpinists and start to appear in climbing
pubs!

Alps 1938 ⟶ | 1959 | The Walker Spur of the Grandes Jorasses is
first climbed by British parties.

Alps 1931 ⟶ | 1961 | First British ascent of N. Face of Matterhorn.

Alps 1932 ⟶ | early 1960s | Helmets, first seen in the Alps, become
popular on British crags and 'front-point'
(12 point) crampons come into general use
by British climbers. The use of climbing
harnesses is seriously mooted following a

Europe ──────→		British death in the Dolomites and the first commercial webbing harness—the 'Tankey' is introduced.
		PAs, first imported privately in the late 1950s—become generally available and their use soon becomes universal for serious rock-climbing.
		MacInnes produces the first 'message'—an all steel ice tool—and a commercial model goes into production.
		Sea-cliff climbing becomes popular and in the ensuing decade many obscure sea-cliffs are discovered and developed. Many peculiar rock types are found to be climbable!
Alps 1938 ──────→	1962	Bonington and Clough make first British ascent of Eigerwand.
Alps mid 1970s ←──		Nuts are first noticed on British crags. By 1964 they are being manufactured commercially and a rapid rise in rock standards results. Later they reach a sceptical USA and Europe.
Alps 1920s ──────→	1963	Crew places the first bolt on Welsh rock—on the Boldest on 'Cloggy'—and climbing ethics are debated in every pub.
		Traverse of the Gods at Swanage resurrects the concept of the long sea-cliff traverse after 50 years.
USA ──────→	1964	First shipments of hard steel pegs arrive from California. American aid techniques and webbing and tape invade the British scene for etrier and slings.
	1966	First climbs are made on Craig Gogarth: the opening of this fierce sea-cliff, climbable at all seasons, leads to another increase in rock-climbing standards.
Alps 1965 ──────→	1967	BBC/TV stage a live 'spectacular' on Orkney's Old Man of Hoy. This highly successful programme does much to stimulate climbing interest and endorses mountaineering as a worthwhile subject in the national media.
		ACG merges with the AC: high standard alpinism has become 'respectable'.
Europe ──────→	late 1960s	Kernmantle rope comes into general use in Britain. There are new developments in ice

		climbing equipment: Chouinard introduces his 'curved' gear and MacInnes his 'Terrordactyl' dropped-pick tools. Tubular ice-screws and wart hogs come into general use and there follows a dramatic upsurge in ice-climbing standards.
Alps early 1970s ←		
Alps early 1970s ←	1969	BMC estimates there are 45,000 'climbers' in Britain of whom 10 per cent visit the Alps. They estimate 500,000 walkers.
USA ← ───────		With the advent of *Mountain* Magazine the English-speaking world has, at last, a regular authorative and professional (and elitist!) international journal of its own. Often climbing opinion reflects that of the magazine.
	early 1970s	Artificial climbing walls proliferate and 'training'—other than on beer—becomes *de rigueur* for serious rock-climbers.
Alps mid 1970s ←	1973	Nicholson solos Zero and Point Five Gullys on Ben Nevis in a morning using the new ice gear: it is a symptom rather than a breakthrough.
	1974	Women are admitted to the Alpine Club.
USA ──────→	mid 1970s	Chalk makes an unwelcome appearance on British crags especially when it is used by mediocre climbers on routes that have been climbed without it.
Alps mid 1970s ← USA		There is a dramatic increase in free climbing standards: top class rock-climbers have become single-minded and dedicated gymnasts—it is a change of attitude. Training, careful preparation and even rehearsal of specific moves, together with great boldness, are now essential before repeating the hardest rock-climbs.
Alps 1961 ──────→	1975	First British winter ascent of Eigerwand.
Alps late 1970s ←	late 1970s	British free climbing standards are reflected in Europe and USA.
USA ← ───────		

The Alps

1492	The first recorded rock-climb: Anthoine de Ville leads his men up Mont Aiguille (6880 ft/2097 m) in the Vercors massif—now in France.

	1786	First ascent of Mont Blanc by Dr Paccard and Jaques Balmat.
	1811	First ascent of Jungfrau by J. and H. Meyer and party.
UK ────────→	1854	Taken as marking the start of the 'Golden Age' of the Alps. In the 11 years to 1865 no less than 180 of the great peaks are first climbed, more than half—all the big prizes —by British parties.
UK ←────────→	1857	With the foundation of the AC mountaineering has become a recognizable 'sport'.
Himalaya 1883 ←───		
	1865	First ascent of the 'Old Brenva'—the Brenva Spur on Mt Blanc's S. Face: it is the first real ice climb.
		First ascent of Matterhorn: the tragedy marks the end of the 'Golden Age'.
UK 1912 ←────	1868	The Swiss Alpine Club (founded 1863) help to build a climbing hut on the Matterhorn: other huts are constructed in the late 1960s.
UK 1894 ←────	1870	Conway publishes his 'Zermatt Pocket Book' —the first Alpine guide book.
Himalaya 1892 ←──		
UK 1907 ←────	1871	Matterhorn becomes an 'easy day for a lady' —first female ascent by Lucy Walker (1835–1916)
Himalaya 1975 ←──		
	1874	First significant winter ascents—those of Jungfrau and Wetterhorn—by W.A. Coolidge, the 'father of winter mountaineering'.
	1870s	Guideless climbing becomes respectable during this decade.
	1878	First ascent of the Aiguille du Dru by Clinton Dent's party: an early ascent of a steep and difficult subsidiary rock peak— symptomatic of a new trend.
UK 1909· ←────	1881	Conway-Coolidge series of pocket guidebooks introduced.
	1906	Winthrop Young with Knubel joins forces with Ryan and the Lochmatters to force the S.W. Face of the Taschhorn—the hardest climb yet made in the Alps. These two teams are currently pioneering alpine routes of a new standard.
Himalaya 1902 ───→	1908	Englishman Oscar Eckenstein redesigns the crampon on sound engineering principles

UK

	c.1910	and promotes its use.
	c.1910	Karabiners are first used by Munich climbers —the idea borrowed from the local fire brigade.
UK 1963 ←————	1920s	Use of pegs, karabiners and 'aid climbing' is being systematically developed by local climbers in the Eastern Alps, although such techniques had been used prior to 1914 by Dülfer and others.
Himalaya 1932 ←—	1924	Ice pegs, invented by Austrian F. Rigele, are first used by Welzenbach on the Grosses Wiesbachhorn in the Hohe Tauern.
Himalaya 1931 ←—	1927	First ascent of the Red Sentinel route on Mont Blanc's Brenva Face by Frank Smythe and T. Graham Brown: it is the first climb on this large and important snow-and-ice face. They climb the Route Major the following year.
UK 1961 ←————	1931	First ascent of Matterhorn N. Face by German Schmid brothers: the 'north wall era' begins in earnest.
UK early 1960s ←—	1932	Grivel invents the 12-point crampon and soon after rigid crampons are being used in Austria.
UK 1951 ←————	1933	Comici climbs the overhanging N. Face of the Cima Grande di Lavaredo in the Dolomites—'aid climbing' has come of age.
UK early 1950s ←—	mid '30s	Vibram soles are invented by Vitale Bramini.
UK 1950 ←————	1935	Frenchman Pierre Allain and Leininger climb the strenuous and steep Dru N. Face and set a new standard on Western Alps rock.
		First ascent of N. Face of Grandes Jorasses: Germans Peters and Maier force the Croz Spur.
UK 1955 ←————	1937	Cassin's party, with a major epic, forces the N.E. Face of the Piz Badile in 52 hours.
UK 1962 ←————	1938	Eiger N. Face—the notorious 'Eigerwand'— is finally climbed by an Austro-German team to whom Hitler presents Olympic gold medals. This fine ascent attracts much bad publicity, especially after several tragic earlier attempts, and the effects took 20 years to live down.

UK 1959 ←		Cassin's Italian team finally climb Walker Spur on Jorasses N. Face.
UK 1947 →	1951	First ascent of E. Face of Grand Capucin, the
UK 1955 ←		first major aid climb in Western Alps: it marks Walter Bonatti's emergence as a 'star' climber.
UK 1954 ←	1952	First ascent of the W. Face of the Aiguille du Dru by a powerful French team in 8 days—a complex and difficult free and aid climb, the most significant of the decade.
Himalaya 1953 ←		Herman Buhl solos the Badile N.E. Face in $4\frac{1}{2}$ hrs—the 10th ascent.
UK late 1950s ←	early 1950s	Down clothing, duvet jackets and pieds d'elephant bags come into general use in the Alps. Bivouacs become pleasant.
	1953	First winter ascent of the Route Major on Mont Blanc's Brenva Face: difficult winter climbing gets under way.
UK 1953 →	1954	Brown and Whillans make 3rd ascent of Dru
UK 1954 →		W. Face in 2 days and subsequently the first ascent of the Blaitiere's Voie Britanique.
	1955	Bonatti makes first ascent of S.W. Pillar— the 'Bonatti Pillar'—of the Dru, solo in 6 days.
	1960	Belgian Claudio Barbier makes solo ascents of all three N. Faces of the Tre Cima di Lavaredo in one day: very hard free and aid climbing accomplished at speed.
UK 1975 ←	1961	First winter ascent of Eigerwand by a German team in 8 days.
		First ascent of Mont Blanc's Central Pillar of Frêney by an Anglo-Polish party. National glory is at stake when a following French party claim for themselves the first ascent of this 'last great problem'. The more unpleasant aspects of modern alpinism are highlighted.
USA →	1962	Americans Hemmings and Robbins add a very difficult direct start to Dru W. Face. It is the first American 'achievement' in the Alps.
USA →	1963	Anglo-American party makes first ascent of S. Face of the Aig. du Fou—probably the hardest technical rock climb in the Alps at

146

the time. American aid techniques are used.
First solo ascent of Eigerwand by Swiss
guide Michel Darbellay in one day.
Bonatti and Zapelli make first ascent of N.
Face of Mt Blanc's Grand Pilier d'Angle—
probably the hardest mixed climb yet made
in the Alps.

1965
Bonatti soloes in winter new direct route on
Matterhorn N. Face in 5 days.
Americans Robbins and Harlin make new
Direct line on Dru W. Face: it demonstrates
American prowess on long and hard rock
climbs.

USA ──────→

UK ──────→
UK 1967 ←──────
Centenary of Whymper's Matterhorn ascent
is celebrated in Zermatt. BBC/TV make a live
broadcast of the Hornli climb and live TV
cameras reach the summit. Mountaineering
has become—briefly—a 'spectator sport'.

1966
A strong Anglo-American-German
consortium forces a Direct Route, in winter,
up the Eigerwand. Siege tactics are used
over 38 days. John Harlin is killed on the
climb.

Himalaya 1970 ←───   1969
Reinhold Messner, already with a name in
the Eastern Alps, appears in the Mont Blanc
massif and solos the great ice wall of Les
Droites N. Face in $8\frac{1}{2}$ hrs—previous best
time is 3 days.

Himalaya 1956 ──→
Japanese climb Eigerwand by new
'Rotefluh' route using siege tactics over 16
days. Many Japanese climbers now visit the
Alps.

UK late 1960s ──→   early
Himalaya 1976 ←──   1970s
The new ice gear appears in the Alps and
dramatically faster ascents of the great ice
routes results.

UK 1969 ──────→
There is a great upsurge in popularity of
alpinism in Europe. Thirty parties bivouac
on Walker Spur one night!

Himalaya 1975 ←──   1974
Messner and Peter Habeler climb Eigerwand
in 10 hrs.

UK 1962 ──────→   mid
Himalaya 1978 ←──   1970s
Technology—the modern ice gear, the
advent of nuts, computerised weather
forecasting—and a change of attitude
resulting from popularity, raises standards

in the Mont Blanc massif. Few climbs are remote any longer.

UK 1973 ⟶ Winter ascents, solo ascents, speed climbing, free ascents of hitherto aid routes and long Russian-style traverses of many peaks become popular. These developments are confined largely to the Mont Blanc massif.

UK late 1970s ⟶
Himalaya 1979 ⟵

late 1970s   The modern attitude in the Alps is that anything goes!

Himalaya and Karakorum

1624   Jesuit priests are the first Europeans to cross the Himalaya—they traverse Garhwal's Mana La (18,400 ft/5600 m) into Tibet.

1830   Alexander Gardiner, travelling from Chinese Turkestan (Sinkiang) to Kashmir, crosses the Karakorum in the vicinity of the Karakorum Pass.

1852   The Survey of India calculates Peak XV— seen only in the distance—to be the world's highest mountain and names it Everest after the late Surveyor-General.

1858   Survey of India calculates the height of K2— still only seen from afar.

1860   Surveyors reach the summit of Shilla (23,050 ft/7026 m) in Punjab Himalaya.

1861   Godwin-Austen, in the course of survey duties, penetrates the heart of the Karakorum and reconnoitres the Biafo and Baltoro Glaciers reaching close to K2.

Alps 1857 ⟶ 1883   W.W. Graham is the first European to visit the Himalaya just to climb '. . . for sport and adventure . . .' as he puts it. He ascends several small peaks in Sikkim and in the Nanda Devi region. He claims an ascent of Changabang! Today we realise that it was possible.

1887   Younghusband, riding from Mongolia to India, crosses the difficult and elusive Mustagh Pass and descends the Baltoro Glacier. Two years later he explores the northern Karakorum descending into Hunza.

Alps 1870 ⟶ 1892   Conway leads an expedition, sponsored by the RGS, to the Karakorum. He traverses the

		Hispar and Biafo Glaciers, explores the Baltoro to its head and ascends Pioneer Peak (22,867 ft/6970 m).
	1895	The first attempt on Nanga Parbat: Mummery, the finest mountaineer of his time, disappears around 20,000 feet (6000 m).
	1899	Freshfield's party makes a complete traverse around the Kangchenjunga massif.
Alps 1908 ←	1902	Britons Oscar Eckenstein and Aleister Crowley lead a first attempt on K2.
	1907	Tom Longstaff's party makes the first ascent of Trisul (23,360 ft/7120 m)—the first seven-thousand-metre peak to be climbed.
	1909	The Duke of Abruzzi's large expedition attempts K2 and reaches 24,600 feet (7500 m) on Chogolisa.
	1921	First reconnaisance of Everest from the north through Tibet: Mallory, Bullock and Wheeler reach the North Col.
	1922	First attempt on Everest: 27,300 feet (8320 m) is reached on the N.E. Ridge.
	1924	Second attempt on Everest: Norton, alone, reaches 28,120 feet (8570 m) without oxygen. Mallory and Irvine are last seen at about 27,600 feet (8400 m) heading towards the summit. There were to be four more British attempts before World War 2 intervened, and climbers include Smythe and Longland.
	1929	A powerful Bavarian expedition attempts Kangchenjunga.
	1930	G.O. Dyhrenfurth leads a strong international team to attempt Kangchenjunga. His son Norman leads a similar international team to Everest 41 years later.
Alps 1927 → UK 1928 →	1931	Frank Smythe's small expedition climbs Kamet (25,447 ft/7756 m): it is the first twenty-five-thousand foot summit to be reached.
Alps 1924 →	1932	A German expedition attempts Nanga Parbat: they return in 1934 and 1937 and 26 men die including the great Welzenbach in the two expeditions.
	1936	A lightweight Anglo-American expedition climbs Nanda Devi (25,645 ft/7817 m).

	1949	Nepal opens its frontiers for the first time.
	1950	Tibet, invaded by the Chinese Communists, becomes forbidden territory.

A French expedition, led by Herzog, climbs Annapurna I: it is the first eight-thousand-metre peak to be climbed.

The following 20 years can be termed the 'Golden Age' of Himalayan climbing as all the great peaks are systematically ascended.

UK 1947 ⟶ 1951 Shipton leads a reconnaisance of the S. side of Everest and discovers a feasible route to the summit.

1952 A Swiss expedition penetrates the Western Cwm of Everest and climbing above the South Col reaches 28,000 feet (8500 m).

1953 A British expedition makes the first ascent of Mount Everest.

Alps 1952 ⟶ An Austro-German expedition is successful on Nanga Parbat. Herman Buhl reaches the summit alone.

1954 The British make the first ascent of Kangchenjunga and the French of Makalu.

Alps 1969 ⟵ 1956 The Japanese make the first ascent of Manaslu and emerge as a major force in Himalayan mountaineering.

UK 1953 ⟶ A lightweight British team make the first ascent of the formidable Mustagh Tower above the Baltoro.

1957 Buhl and his Austrian friends climb Broad Peak (26,400 ft/8047 m) in alpine style. This significant ascent is the first use of such tactics on an eight-thousand-metre peak: it is the shape of things to come.

1961 Due to political problems the Pakistan Government closes the Baltoro region of the Karakorum. It is to remain forbidden until 1974.

1963 Hornbein and Unsoeld of the lavish American expedition climb the W. Ridge to complete the first traverse—and the first 'new route' —on Everest. This climb must rank with the greatest Himalayan achievements ever.

1964 The Chinese climb Shisha Pangma (Gosainthan)—the last of the eight-

thousand-metre peaks.

1965 Nepal closes its mountains to climbers.

1969 Nepal opens its mountains again and announces new 'mountaineering rules' and a very restricted list of 'permitted peaks'. Commercial trekking gets under way in Nepal: the tourist boom that develops over the next five years enables small parties to visit the Himalaya easily and cheaply.

1970 A powerful British expedition climbs the S. Face of Annapurna—setting a new standard of difficulty on big mountains and emphasising the start of a new era in the Himalaya when the route is more important than the summit.

Alps 1969 ⟶ Climbing with a German-Tyrolese expedition on Nanga Parbat, the Messner brothers ascend the virgin Rupal Face but are forced to descend the Diamir Face thus making—unintentionally—the first traverse of the mountain.

Alps 1871 ⟶ 1975 A Japanese woman reaches the summit of Everest.

Despite previous dubious claims the Chinese now definitely reach the summit of Everest via the N.E. Ridge.

Alps 1974 ⟶ Reinhold Messner and Peter Habeler climb Hidden Peak (26,470 ft/8068 m) in a single 3 day alpine-style push: it is a two-man expedition.

Lavishly financed and fully commercialised, a strong British team finally climbs the S.W. Face of Everest after 6 previous expeditions had failed. It proves to be easier than imagined. For the British this controversial expedition is the 'last of the dinosaurs' but for many countries the ascent of Everest has become a national status symbol and the mountain is booked solid for years to come.

Alps early 1970s ⟶ 1976 Two Britons with no support force the W. Face of Changabang after 25 days of exceptionally difficult mixed climbing. It is perhaps the most technical climb in the Himalaya to date.

	1977	A New Zealand team attempts Everest without sherpa assistance: in a brave effort they reach the South Col. It is symptomatic of a new approach to Himlayan climbing as other parties attempt big mountains unassisted.
	1978	Messner and Habeler, climbing with an Austro-German expedition, reach the summit of Everest without oxygen. A blaze of publicity accompanies this now relatively insignificant feat.
Alps mid 1970s ⟶		Later Messner climbs the Diamir flank of Nanga Parbat entirely solo—a 'one-man-expedition'—in 12 days. In the context of Himalayan history this is a far more important achievement than his Everest ascent.
		The Nepalese Government publishes a new 'permitted list' containing many hitherto forbidden but highly desirable virgin peaks.
Alps late 1970s ⟶	1979	A four-man Anglo-French party attempts a new route on Kangchenjunga. Scott, Boardman and Tasker reach the summit in semi-alpine style using no oxygen or porters. It is a tour-de-force in the new idiom.
Alps mid 1970s ⟶	1980	Nepalese Government announces that winter expeditions will now be permitted thus recognizing three climbing seasons.

How to Start

All mountain activities are, to a greater or lesser extent, 'risk sports'. As such, the skills that are demanded for their safe practice should be learnt properly. Experience however, can only be gained the hard way and it is wise to gain it in the company of a more experienced mentor. While many great climbers are entirely self-taught, it is a good plan to join a local club where beginners are welcomed or to take a course at a specialist mountain school. Edward Whymper's famous warning, though rather dire, is as applicable today as it was when mountaineering was young: 'Climb if you will but remember that courage and strength are nought without prudence. . . . Do nothing in haste, look well to each step, and from the beginning think what may be the end.'

The following organisations should be able to help you:
(some addresses are liable to change)
BRITISH MOUNTAINEERING COUNCIL
Crawford House, Precinct Centre, Booth Street East, Manchester M13 9RZ
MOUNTAINEERING COUNCIL OF SCOTLAND
(Hon.Sec.) 59 Morningside Park, Edinburgh.
FEDERATION OF MOUNTAINEERING CLUBS OF IRELAND
(Hon.Sec.) 7 Sorbonne, Ardilea Estate, Dublin 14.
THE SPORTS COUNCIL NATIONAL MOUNTAINEERING CENTRE
Plas y Brenin, Capel Curig, Gwynedd, North Wales.
THE SCOTTISH SPORTS COUNCIL NATIONAL MOUNTAIN CENTRE
Glenmore Lodge, Aviemore, Highland.
NATIONAL SKI FEDERATION OF GREAT BRITAIN
c/o Ski Club of Great Britain, 118 Eaton Square, London SW1 W9AF.
FELL RUNNERS ASSOCIATION
(Hon.Sec.) 127 Bury Road, Rawtenstall, Rossendale, Lancs.
BACKPACKERS CLUB
(Hon.Sec.) 20 St Michaels Road, Tilehurst, Reading, Berks RG3 4RP.
VENTURING LTD (for trekking)
49 Conduit Street, London W1R 9FB.

AUSTRALIAN CLIMBING UNION
Sydney.
ALPINE CLUB OF CANADA
P.O. box 1026, Banff, Alberta.
INDIAN MOUNTAINEERING FEDERATION
Ministry of Defence, 18 'Q' block, New Delhi.
HIMALAYAN CLUB
(Hon.Sec.) P.O. Box 1905, Bombay 400 001, India.
MOUNTAIN TRAVEL (INDIA) PVT LTD,
189 Jorbagh, New Delhi—110003, India.
KONINKLIJKE NEDERLANDSE ALPENVEREINGUNG
Wassernaarseweg 220, Postbus 2200, s'Gravenhage, Holland.
CLUB ALPIN ISRAELIEN
Bd Rothschild 60, Tel-Aviv, Israel.
JAPANESE ALPINE CLUB
Sunview Building, 5/4 Yonban-cho, Chiyoda-ku, Tokyo 102.
MOUNTAIN CLUB OF KENYA
P.O. Box 5741, Nairobi. (MCK Building, Wilson Aerodrome, Nairobi)
NEPAL MOUNTAINEERING ASSOCIATION
Sports Council Building, Kathmandu.
MOUNTAIN TRAVEL (NEPAL) LTD.,
P.O. Box 170, Kathmandu.
NEW ZEALAND ALPINE CLUB
P.O. Box 41–038, Eastbourne, near Wellington.
NORSK TINDEKLUB,
Post Boks 1727, Vika, Oslo 1. Norway.
PAKISTAN ALPINE CLUB
Rawalpindi.
MOUNTAIN CLUB OF SOUTH AFRICA,
P.O. Box 164, Cape Town.
SVENSKA KLATTERFORBUNDET,
P.O. Box 14036, 70014 Orebro, Sweden.
AMERICAN ALPINE CLUB
113 East 90th Street, New York, N.Y. 10028.
SIERRA CLUB
530 Bush Street, San Francisco, California 94108. USA.
MOUNTAIN TRAVEL (USA) INC.,
1398 Solano Avenue, Albany, California 94706.

Glossary

Aid climbing   Artificial climbing: progress using gadgets such as pegs, expansion-bolts, nuts etc, for direct-aid on rock or ice where free climbing is not possible. In theory, with enough effort and rock of any quality, no climb is impossible using aid tactics.

Aiguille   French word for 'needle': used in the Alps, especially in the Mont Blanc Range, and now elsewhere in the world, to describe a sharp pointed mountain—usually a rock peak.

Alpine, Alpine Style, Alpine Fashion   Similar to the European Alps—in height, in snow and ice cover, in terrain. The kind of climbing practised in the Alps (see chapter *Alpine Climbing*). The technique of rope management in which two or more climbers move simultaneously, one or other taking an instantaneous belay on a rock or dug-in ice axe.

Arete   A narrow or knife-edged ridge or rock-feature—it may be horizontal or vertical.

Belay, to belay   An attachment, or point of attachment, to the rock or ice for security purposes. To secure the active—or moving—rope of one's colleague, usually around one's own body, itself attached to a belay, in such a way as virtually to lock it in the event of a fall.

Bergschrund   Also 'Schrund or Rimaye. The crevasse between ice slopes, and/or rock, moving in a different direction or angle. Typically the serious obstacle between a glacier and its containing rock wall or ice slope above.

Big-wall climbing   A style of climbing typically used on the largest and blankest rock faces where multi-day ascents, specialised rope techniques and hanging bivouacs are needed. Originally developed in Yosemite and—on very big mountains—the essence of 'Capsule' techniques. See chapters *Rock Climbing, High Altitude Mountaineering*.

Chimney   A vertical fissure in a rock face, wider than a crack but narrower than a gully and large enough for a man to get into.

Col   A saddle or dip in a ridge, usually between two mountains: sometimes, but not always, a pass.

Cornice   An overhanging curl of snow or snow-ice usually along one side of a ridge crest or plateau edge and often overhanging many feet. It is formed by wind action.

Couloir   A gully, usually a snow or ice gully, on a big mountain.

Crampon   A steel frame with downward pointing spikes about 2 inches (5 cm) long which fits closely to the sole of the climbing boot and is used for ice climbing or moving over verglassed rock. Originally, as developed by Oscar Eckenstein, with 10 points, but nowadays having in addition 2 forward pointing (lobster) claws.

Cwm, Corrie, Cirque   Welsh word describing a small hanging valley holding—or once holding—a small glacier. Sometimes the blind head of a valley.

Deadman, Deadboy, Deadbaby   A snow anchor, a flat alloy plate—maybe one foot square or smaller—with a wire loop attached in the centre. Difficult to place correctly but, driven or pushed into soft snow, provides an excellent belay.

Exposure   That psychological factor, to which height above the ground, distance from safety and steepness all contribute, which makes a given move on rock or ice more difficult than it would be at ground level.

Fell   Mountain, hill or high moorland in northern England.

Free climbing   Progress without using artificial aids: on rocks using only the natural holds and on ice using only the accepted techniques of crampons, axe and hammers. Definitely not the use of pegs.

Fixed rope   A rope or line fixed over a difficult move, pitch or slope. May be used merely as a hand rail or for direct aid or it may be climbed hanging completely free over an overhang using special rope climbing gadgets (jumars). An important part of siege tactics. See chapter *High Altitude Mountaineering*.

Gendarme   A tower or pinnacle on a ridge which impedes progress—literally 'a policeman barring the way'.

Girdle   A traverse, especially the horizontal traverse of a cliff.

Glissade   The technique of sliding down steep slopes of hardish snow on the boot soles and under control—a sort of 'poor man's skiing'.

Grade   A system used to describe the difficulty of a climb. Many concurrent systems are in use and are usually confusing, conflicting and controversial! On alpine mountains the French and British favour the 'Vallot' system which takes into account the length, seriousness and objective dangers of a route with an overall adjectival grade such as 'Assez Difficile' (AD) through 'Difficile' (D) and 'Tres Difficile' (TD) to 'Extremement Difficile' (ED) and then adds a numerical grade to cover the technical difficulty of the hardest individual pitches in normal conditions on a scale I to VI. Thus the Eigerwand is graded 'ED with several pitches of V' while the West Flank, the 'voie normale', is considered merely 'PD' (Peu Difficile). Aid pitches are grades A1 to A4. On British rock two basic systems operate: an adjectival system of Moderate (M), Difficult (D), Very Difficult (VD), Severe (S) and Extreme (XS), and a numerical system 1 to 6 with subdivisions of a, b and c which is usually reserved for outcrops or individual pitches. On Scottish ice a numerical system is again used which considers the commitment as well as the difficulty of a climb and bears no relationship to any other numerical system. For instance Grade 1 is a straightforward snow climb with no ice pitches but possibly mild cornice difficulties at the top, while Grade V covers a long sustained climb of greatest difficulty requiring a powerful party and favourable conditions—although probably no harder technically than Grade 1V.

Several systems are used in America, best known being the logical though often superfluous Californian Decimal System. Thus 'Class 3' is scrambling with no rope, 'Class 4' requires a rope and 'Class 5' requires protection too and is subdivided into 5.1 to 5.9 and further. Thus a 5.7 pitch, if soloed, reverts to 'Class 3' whatever its technical difficulty! A further 'Grade' of I–VI covers the length and seriousness of the climb, so that a single pitch boulder problem of 5.10 would be Grade I while a serious multi-day big-wall would be Grade VI. A very sensible system of cardinal numbers is used on Australian rock climbs.

An approximate comparison is:

Britain		USA	Australia	Alpine
Hard severe	4b	5.6	12–13	V
Very severe	4c	5.7	14–15	V+
Hard VS	5a	5.8	16–17	VI
Extreme	5b	5.9	18–19	VI+
Extreme	6a	5.11	22	probably Aid

Greater Mountaineering Climbing on big mountains of alpine scale or more—usually the really great ranges of the world.

Gully, Ghyll An erosion-formed fissure or rift, usually rocky, running downwards on a face or mountain flank. It may be wide or narrow, an easy walk or a difficult climb.

Hypothermia Sometimes called 'Exposure'—a medical condition sometimes fatal when body heat is lost more rapidly than produced.

Ice Bollard A knob or bollard carved from ice as a belay.

Ice Fall A section of extremely tortured ice, with huge crevasses and seracs, formed where a glacier flows over a steep step in its bed. Because the glacier is moving the ice is extremely unstable and dangerous.

Ice Screw A modern form of ice peg threaded for easy retrieval—may be of corkscrew form or tubular. See also *Wart Hog* and *Peg*.

Inseleberg   A peculiar rock formation: an isolated rock spire or pinnacle rising steeply from the surrounding flat country.

Jumar   A special metal clamp which will slide up a rope but not down it: a generic term often now used to describe other than just the original Jumar itself. Two are used to climb a hanging rope.

Karabiner, Krab   A snap-link with a spring-loaded gate usually made of light alloy and used for a wide range of attachment purposes.

Kernmantle   A modern method of rope construction in which the individual filaments lie straight and are tightly covered with a woven sheath—as opposed to the traditional twisted or 'hawser-laid' rope.

Matterhorn Peak   A sharp pyramidical mountain whose several steep aretes have been formed by the glacial erosion of the intervening faces —the Matterhorn is the prime example.

Mesa   A flat topped table-mountain, a plateau with steep sides, a butte.

Mixed ground, Mixed climbing   Terrain on which rock is mixed with snow and ice. Mixed climbing often necessitates negotiating rock moves while wearing crampons.

New Zealand foot brake   A belay method for hard snow and ice in which the rope running around the belayer's foot tends to lock his crampon points into the ice.

Nut, Chock   A small artificial chock-stone, originally an engineer's nut but nowadays a specially designed metal or plastic wedge, which is cunningly inserted into a crack in such a way that it cannot be pulled out in the direction of any likely loading. The use of nuts for protection has revolutionised free climbing and they are now often used in place of pegs.

Orienteering   A Scandinavian national sport now popular in Britain in which competitors race cross-country via a series of check-points which can be located only by sophisticated map-and-compass navigation.

Outcrop   Taken to mean, in Britain, the lesser rocks—even quarries— outside the mountain areas on which rock-climbing can be practised: may be 20 feet (6 m) or as much as 200 feet (60 m) high.

P.A.   Originally a highly specialised lightweight canvas and rubber climbing bootee with a smooth hard rubber sole designed by French guide and equipment manufacturer Pierre Allain: now a generic term used to describe many such 'magic boots' on the market.

Parallel skiing   A ski technique in which both ski remain parallel throughout the turning manoeuvre.

Peg, Piton   A steel blade with an eye in its head in various forms, shapes and sizes, which is hammered into a crack either for security or as an aid to progress.

Pendule   A horizontal move made by swinging on the rope like a pendulum, used to cross otherwise holdless rock.

Piste   French word, literally track or trail. Used to describe a trail carved through snow by previous skiers or the footsteps of climbers.

Pitch   Section of a climb, usually of some 60–150 feet (18–45 m), between ledges or belay points. A 'lead'—the distance a leader will climb before stopping to bring up his second man.

Rappel, Abseil   Roping-down: a means of descent by sliding down a rope under the control of the friction either of the rope passing around the body or through a gadget of some kind clipped to the waist.

Rope   A team of climbers all roped together, usually two or three.

Runner, Running-belay   Protection: a point of attachment to the rock or ice, usually using a natural rock-spike, a nut or a peg together with a sling, through which the climbing rope runs freely via a karabiner. Several 'runners' may be used at convenient places on a pitch. See chapter *Rock Climbing*.

'Schrund   See Bergschrund.

Scree, Talus   Rock detritus, ranging in size from small stones to fairly large boulders, lying loosely on a slope having fallen from crags above. Can be tiresome to ascend or descend.

Self arrest, Ice axe brake   Technique of arresting a slide, probably accidental and uncontrolled, down snow or ice slopes, using the pick of the ice-axe.

Serac   An ice cliff, a tower of ice as occurs in an Ice-fall. Always unstable and thus dangerous.

Sherpa   Member of a Nepali mountain tribe of Tibetan origin and Bhuddist religion who inhabit the Solu-Khumbu region at the foot of, and to the south of Mt Everest. They were first recruited as mountain porters in Darjeeling at the turn of the century when Dr A.M. Kellas, a noted Himalayan pioneer, discovered some likely fellows working in the bazaar. Their subsequent performance at high altitude, their dependability, cheerfulness and natural charm—particularly on the early Everest expeditions—established for them a high reputation and an essential role in expeditionary mountaineering. Always good companions, they have today developed from being mere high altitude porters to become excellent cooks, trekking guides and summit climbers in their own right. Natural traders and entrepreneurs, and now closely involved in the tourist business, they are probably the most affluent mountain tribe in the world. The term 'sherpa' is often used in a generic sense to describe 'supporting climbers' of any nationality.

Sling   A loop of rope or nylon tape with a multitude of uses.

Siege tactics   See chapter *High Altitude Mountaineering*. Such tactics are not confined to really large mountains but have been used in the Alps, for example on the first ascent of the Eiger Direct, and in Yosemite during the first ascent of the Nose of El Capitan, and elsewhere.

Stack   An isolated pinnacle, usually rising from the sea or foreshore. Britain's highest stack is Stac an Armin (627 ft/191 m) off St Kilda.

Stance   A belay ledge on which a climber can adopt the best position to hold a fall from either above or below : or the position itself.

Three point contact   Moving only one hand or foot at a time so that the climber is on three holds at any one moment.

Top Rope, Top Roping   A rope from above : a rope security method used on outcrops when a climb is not led, the belayer is either at the crag top or at the bottom with the rope returning to him via a runner at the top.

Traverse   A series of sideways moves, a horizontal section of climbing, the crossing of a mountain—or series of mountains—by ascending one side and descending by another.

Trek, Trekking   Originally the approach march to a large mountain, the journey to Base Camp. As an 'adventure holiday' first marketed on a commercial basis by Col. Jimmy Roberts—the well-known Himalayan explorer and mountaineer—and his company Mountain Travel in Nepal in the mid-1960s. Now a very popular activity throughout the Himalaya—and in the Karakorum, the Andes, Africa and elsewhere—enabling walkers with little previous experience to visit and journey through high mountain country in comfort and safety under an expert leader and with properly organised logistics.

Tyrolean traverse   A traverse made by climbing along a rope fixed at either end. Originally used in the Tyrol where an otherwise inaccesible pinnacle was lasooed from the summit of an adjacent peak.

Vibram   A moulded and cleated rubber sole developed by Vitale Bramani in the 1930s and used on the first ascents of the Jorasses' Walker Spur and the North Face of the Dru. The name is, in fact, a registered trade mark, but as such soles are universal on climbing, mountain and walking boots, it has become generic.

Verglas   A thin film of ice covering rock, often a temporary condition.

Voie normale   French word, the regular route, the usual way. Probably the easiest route, but certainly the easiest practical and safe route.

Wart Hog   A non-tubular ice peg with a broken thread so that it can be easily and swiftly hammered straight into the ice yet removed easily by un-screwing.

Wax   Special waxes are used on the base of ski to make them run easily. On nordic ski the correct wax for the prevailing conditions of snow temperature and humidity enables the ski to grip for propulsion and yet to glide when running. Nordic waxing has become an art.

Acknowledgements

The author and publisher would like to acknowledge the contribution made by Audrey Salkeld in the preparation of Chapters 3 and 4.

The photographs have been taken mainly by the author but particular acknowledgement for the others is made to: Alex Bertulis, p. 41; Herman Wolf, p. 44; Ned Kelly, p. 46; Doug Scott, p. 48; Jim Stuart, p. 54 (bottom right).

Bibliography

It has been claimed that mountaineering has produced the biggest literature of any sport: these are some of the books that are especially relevant to this present volume.

Ahluwalia, Major H.P.S. (1978) *Faces of Everest*: Vikas, New Delhi.

Azema, M. (1957) *The Conquest of Fitzroy*: Deutsch, London.

Bell, J.H.B. (1950) *A Progress in Mountaineering*: Oliver & Boyd.

Benuzzi, Felice (1952) *No Picnic on Mount Kenya*: William Kimber.

Boardman, Peter (1978) *The Shining Mountain*: Hodder & Stoughton.

Bonington, Chris (1966) *I Chose to Climb*: Gollancz.

(1973) *The Next Horizon*: Gollancz.

(1976) *Everest, The Hard Way*: Hodder & Stoughton.

Brown, Joe (1967) *The Hard Years*: Gollancz.

Buhl, Herman (1956) *Nanga Parbat Pilgrimage*: Hodder & Stoughton.

Clark, Ronald (1977) *Men Myths & Mountains*: Weidenfeld & Nicholson.

Clark, Ronald and Pyatt, Ted (1957) *Mountaineering in Britain*: Phoenix House.

Cleare, John (1979) *World Guide to Mountains*: Collins.

(1975) *Mountains*: Macmillan.

Cleare, John and Collomb, Robin (1973) *Sea Cliff Climbing in Britain*: Constable.

Cleare, John and Smythe, Tony (1966) *Rock Climbers in Action in Snowdonia*: Secker & Warburg.

Davidson, Art (1969) *Minus 148: The Winter Ascent of Mt McKinley*: W.W. Norton, New York.

Diemberger, Kurt (1971) *Summits and Secrets*: Allen & Unwin.

Gray, Dennis (1970) *Rope Boy*: Gollancz.

Harrer, H. (1959, 1976) *The White Spider*: Hart-Davis.

Haston, Dougal (1972) *In High Places*: Cassell.

Jones, Chris (1976) *Climbing in North America*: American Alpine Club, N.Y.

Keay, John (1977) *Where Men and Mountains Meet*: John Murray.

(1979) *The Gilgit Game*: John Murray.

Longstaff, Tom (1950) *This my Voyage*: John Murray.

MacInnes, Hamish (1974) *Climb to the Lost World*: Hodder & Stoughton.

Mason, Kenneth (1955) *Abode of Snow:* Hart-Davis.

Messner, Reinhold (1977) *The Challenge, Two Men Alone at 8,000 Metres:* Kaye & Ward.

Messner, Reinhold (1980) *Solo — Nanga Parbat 1978:* Kaye & Ward.

Mummery, A.F. *My Climbs in the Alps and Caucasus:* Fisher Unwin, 1895. Blackwell, Oxford, 1936. Quarterman, USA, 1974.

Murray. W.H. (1979) *Mountaineering in Scotland, Undiscovered Scotland:* Diadem.

Noyce, W. and McMorrin, Ian (1969) *World Atlas of Mountaineering:* Nelson.

Patey, Tom (1971) *One Man's Mountains:* Gollancz.

Pearse, R.O. (1973) *Barrier of Spears — Drama of the Drakensberg:* Howard Timmins, Cape Town.

Rebuffat, Gaston (1968) *Starlight and Storm:* Kaye & Ward.
                  (1974) *Mont Blanc Massif — 100 Best Routes:* Kaye & Ward.

Roberts, D. (1968) *Mountain of My Fear:* Vanguard Press, New York.

Rowell, Galen (1977) *In the Throne Room of the Mountain Gods:* Allen & Unwin.

Shipton, Eric (1969) *That Untravelled World:* Hodder & Stoughton.
              (1947) *Upon That Mountain:* Hodder & Stoughton.

Steck, Allen and Roper, Steve (1979) *50 Classic Climbs of North America:* Sierra Club, San Francisco.

Whillans, Don (1971) *Portrait of a Mountaineer:* Heinemann.

Whymper, Edward (1871, 1965) *Scrambles Amongst the Alps:* Murray.

Wilson, Ken (ed) (1978) *Games Climbers Play:* Diadem.

Tobias, Mike and Drasdo, Harold (1979) *The Mountain Spirit:* Overlook Press, New York.

Tilman, H.W. (1937) *The Ascent of Nanda Devi:* Cambridge U.P.

Smythe, Frank (1940) *Adventures of a Mountaineer:* Dent.
             (1957) *Climbs and Ski Runs:* A&C Black.

Young, G. Winthrop (1920) *Mountain Craft:* Methuen.
                   (1927) *On High Hills:* Methuen.
                   (1951) *Mountains With a Difference:* Eyre & Spottiswoode.

Steele, Peter (1972) *Doctor on Everest:* Hodder & Stoughton.

The following books are especially noteworthy because of their pictures:

Clark, Ronald (1948) *The Splendid Hills, The Photographs of Vittorio Sella:* Phoenix House.

Chouinard, Yvon (1949) *Climbing Ice:* Sierra Club, San Francisco.

Hagen, Toni (1961) *Nepal:* Kummerly & Frey.

Harris & Hasler (1972) *A Land Apart* (New Zealand Alps): Reed, New Zealand.

Hornbein, Tom (1966) *Everest, The West Ridge:* Sierra Club, San Francisco.

Rebuffat, Gaston (1956) *Mont Blanc to Everest:* Thames & Hudson.

Roch, Andre (1947) *On Rock and Ice:* A&C Black.

Shirakawa, Y. (1976) *Himalayas:* Harry Abrams, New York.

Pause, W. and Winkler, J. (1979) *Extreme Alpine Rock:* Granada.

Wilson, Ken (1975) *Hard Rock:* Granada.

        (1978) *Classic Rock:* Granada.

The following are 'how-to-do-it' books and will give important background to the chapters on *Mountain Sports* in the present volume:

Blackshaw, Alan (1965, 1975) *Mountaineering, From Hill Walking to Alpine Climbing:* Penguin.

Langmuir, Eric (1969) *Mountain Leadership:* S.C.P.R. Edinburgh.

Livesey, Peter (1978) *Rock Climbing:* E.P. Sport.

MacInnes, Hamish (1972) *International Mountain Rescue Handbook:* Constable.

March, Bill (1976) *Modern Snow and Ice Techniques:* Cicerone Press, Manchester.

March, Bill (1976) *Modern Rope Techniques in Mountaineering:* Cicerone.

Paulcke and Dumler (1973) *Hazards in Mountaineering:* Kaye & Ward.

Rebuffat, Gaston (1971) *On Ice and Snow and Rock:* Kaye & Ward.

Robbins, Royal (1971) *Basic Rockcraft:* La Siesta Press, California.

        (1973) *Advanced Rockcraft:* La Siesta Press.

Scott, Doug (1974) *Big Wall Climbing:* Kaye & Ward.

Ski Club of Great Britain (1961) *Handbook on Ski Touring* & *Glacier Skiing:* Ski Club of G.B. London.

Steele, Peter (1976) *Medical Care for Mountain Climbers:* Heinemann Medical.

Tejada-Flores, Lito and Steck, Allen (1972) *Wilderness Skiing:* Sierra Club, San Francisco.

Index

The figures in **bold** refer to colour plates. Those in italics refer to the page numbers of black and white illustrations. Other figures refer to text pages. Mountains and Ranges have been listed under names rather than such prefixes as: Ben, Cordillera, Mont, Pik, etc.

165